THE ART QUIZ BOOK

2000+ QUESTIONS ON PAINTERS AND PAINTINGS

Colin J. Bailey

THE ART QUIZ BOOK
2000+ Questions on Painters and Paintings

© Colin J. Bailey 1995

The right of Colin J. Bailey to be identified as the author of this work has been asserted by him in accordance with the Copyright, Designs and Patents Act 1988.

British Library Cataloguing in Publication Data. A catalogue record for this book is available from the British Library

ISBN 0 9524342 1 0

Published by Station Press Ltd, 10 Links Place, Port Seton, East Lothian, EH32 0TP, Scotland, U.K.

Printed by The Edinburgh Press Ltd

CONTENTS

For my students: past, present, and future

INTRODUCTION

Long-running television series such as Mastermind, University Challenge and Blockbusters; successful radio programmes like Brain of Britain and Round Britain Quiz; and the perennially popular board game Trivial Pursuit prove that most of us, whatever our age, enjoy putting our knowledge and memory to the test and pitting our wits against others, including the acknowledged experts.

Few of us compete at home against the Mastermind contestants in the realistic expectation of doing better than the people answering questions on their specialist subjects. We derive our enjoyment from the radio and television programmes not simply because they challenge us but also because, in the process of participation, we are educated and entertained.

The Art Quiz Book has been devised with three main purposes in mind. First and foremost, it is intended to enable anyone with an interest in art, from the occasional gallery visitor to the professional art historian, to discover how much he or she really knows and is able to recall about painters and painting from the Renaissance to the present. It can be used to test yourself or be inflicted on others. Its second aim is to inform and educate by introducing questions to which you may not already know the answers. I have learned much from compiling The Art Quiz Book, and I hope, when you have reached the end, that you too will feel that your own store of knowledge has been enriched. The third aim of The Art Quiz Book is to divert and entertain. Many of the two thousand questions have been included not because people will necessarily know the answers, or that the questions are particularly important, but because they involve amusing anecdotes or convey little-known but curious facts. Because the quiz book slips easily into a handbag or a coat pocket, it may be used for ready reference in galleries and exhibitions.

The Art Quiz Book is divided into three sections headed Student, Connoisseur and Genius. Broadly speaking, the earliest questions are the simplest and the last questions the most difficult, but what some will find hard others may find easy and, anyway, the memory plays strange tricks. If you score between eight and fourteen in any group of twenty-five questions, you have done well; if you score more than fifteen, you have both excellent knowledge and a phenomenal memory; if you score twenty-five out of twenty-five, you clearly have the calibre of a mastermind. Those of you wishing to start at the 'shallow end', will be gratified to find several series of questions with multiple-choice answers.

If you are undecided as to whether to buy The Art Quiz Book, see if you can answer question 5 on page 98. If you cannot, then you *need* to buy it! If, on the other hand, you can answer correctly every question on page 101 and page 102, you should perhaps consider buying it for someone else! You could then ask them to test you, which would allow you to show off. If you enjoy a challenge, enter the prize competition on page 127.

Whatever your motives for buying The Art Quiz Book, I hope it will provide you with hours of entertainment and not drive you mad when you cannot recall the answer *you know* you know so well.

Colin J. Bailey
Edinburgh, September 1995

ACKNOWLEDGEMENTS

The idea of writing The Art Quiz Book occurred to me some three years ago and it was completed during my summer vacation in 1993. From the outset I have received support and encouragement from colleagues and friends alike, and it is my very pleasant duty to record my heartfelt thanks to them here.

For allowing themselves to be used as guinea pigs, I should like to thank particularly my colleagues in the Department of Humanities at Edinburgh College of Art, to whom I am indebted for so much else besides.

Once the book was finished, MaryAnne Stevens at the Royal Academy did more than anyone else at that time to convince me of its educational value. Her early encouragement sustained me during the lengthy process of finding a publisher.

Eventually, by a strange turn of fate, it was one of my final year students, Tamara Clarke, who suggested I contact Tony Harrison of the Station Press.

Tony was enthusiastic about The Art Quiz Book from the very beginning, and it has been a genuine pleasure working with someone so professional, hardworking and committed.

Ever sympathetic to my wishes as author, Tony nevertheless made a number of recommendations which have significantly benefitted the final version of the book, including the incorporation of colour and black and white reproductions.

For permission to reproduce the works in their care, I am grateful to the Trustees and Directors of the following museums and art galleries:-   The Barber Institute of Fine Arts, The University of Birmingham; The City Museum and Art Gallery, Birmingham; The National Galleries of Scotland, Edinburgh; Glasgow Museums: The Burrell Collection; The Walker Art Gallery, Liverpool; The National Gallery, London; The Tate Gallery, London; City Art Galleries, Manchester; and the Ashmolean Museum, Oxford.

For their personal assistance, I wish to thank Ian Charlton, Richard Clark, Carlotta Gelmetti, Deborah Hunter, Edward Morris, Winnie Tyrrell, Richard Verdi, Tracy Walker, and, above all, John Leighton.

Colin J. Bailey

Section One

STUDENT

Fig. 1 "The Rest on the Flight into Egypt" by Orazio Gentileschi
Birmingham Museum and Art Gallery

By which British artists were the following painted:

1. "And when did you last see your father?"
2. "The Blind Girl"
3. "Hadleigh Castle"
4. "The Scapegoat"
5. "The Last of England"
6. "The Death of General Gordon"
7. "Home from Sea"
8. "Dignity and Impudence"
9. "Sadak in Search of the Waters of Oblivion"
10. "Applicants for Admission to a Casual Ward"
11. "Cimabue's celebrated Madonna is carried in Procession through the Streets of Florence"
12. "The Fairy Feller's Master-Stroke"
13. "The Death of Chatterton"
14. The "Pelican Portrait" of Elizabeth I
15. "Found"
16. "Derby Day"
17. "Snowstorm: Hannibal and his Army crossing the Alps"
18. "A Hopeless Dawn"
19. "The Last Day in the Old Home"
20. "Pitlessie Fair"
21. "Hope"
22. "Omnibus Life in London"
23. "The Light of the World"
24. "Laus Veneris"
25. "Solomon Eagle exhorting the People to Repentance during the Plague of London"

Who painted:

The answers have been mixed up - can you match the questions and answers?

1.	"The Ghent Altarpiece"	William Dyce
2.	"The Ognissanti Madonna"	Andrea Mantegna
3.	"The Canigiani Holy Family"	Parmigianino
4.	"The Embarkation from Cythera"	Jean-Honoré Fragonard
5.	"An Experiment on a Bird in an Air Pump"	John Constable
6.	"The Blue Boy"	William Hogarth
7.	"The Bather of Valpinçon"	Hubert(?) and Jan van Eyck
8.	"The Death of Sardanapalus"	Diego Velazquez
9.	"The Triumphs of Caesar"	Giotto
10.	"The Romans of the Decadence"	Edwin Landseer
11.	"The Rokeby Venus"	Vincent van Gogh
12.	"Les Parapluies"	Antoine Watteau
13.	"The Kiss"	Paulus Potter
14.	"The Nightmare"	Thomas Gainsborough
15.	"The Young Bull"	Jean François Millet
16.	"Pegwell Bay, Kent"	Thomas Couture
17.	"La Mariée mise à nu par ses célibataires, même"	Eugène Delacroix
18.	"The Gleaners"	Gustav Klimt
19.	"The Madonna of the Long Neck"	Raphael
20.	"The Swing"	Jean-Auguste-Dominique Ingres
21.	"The Cornfield"	Joseph Wright of Derby
22.	"The Stag at Bay"	Duccio di Buoninsegna
23.	"The Potato Eaters"	Marcel Duchamp
24.	"The Rucellai Madonna"	Henry Fuseli (Johann Heinrich Füssli)
25.	"The Shrimp Girl"	Pierre Auguste Renoir

With which towns are the following most closely associated:

Select the correct answer from the three alternatives given

1. Frans Hals — Haarlem / Amsterdam / Rotterdam

2. Hans Memlinc — Ghent / Frankfurt / Bruges

3. Jan Vermeer — Amsterdam / Leiden / Delft

4. Hugo van der Goes — Brussels / Ghent / Liège

5. Rogier van der Weyden — Brussels / Ghent / Bruges

6. Peter Paul Rubens — Antwerp / Paris / Amsterdam

7. Albrecht Dürer — Augsburg / Regensburg / Nuremberg

8. Albrecht Altdorfer — Munich / Regensburg / Augsburg

9. Vittore Carpaccio — Mantua / Venice / Pisa

10. El Greco — Madrid / Toledo / Barcelona

11. Diego Velazquez — Barcelona / Cadiz / Madrid

12. Franz Marc — Munich / Dresden / Berlin

13. Caspar David Friedrich — Dresden / Berlin / Leipzig

14. Dieric Bouts — Bruges / Brussels / Louvain

15. Hendrick Terbrugghen — Utrecht / The Hague / Delft

16. Antonio Correggio — Florence / Siena / Parma

17. Cosmè Tura — Naples / Rome / Ferrara

18. Vincent van Gogh — Arles / Bordeaux / Nîmes

19. Stephan Lochner — Weimar / Cologne / Düsseldorf

20. Claude Lorraine — Paris / Rome / Florence

21. Vincenzo Foppa — Milan / Mantua / Ferrara

22. Bartolommeo Manfredi — Urbino / Arezzo / Mantua

23. Pietro Longhi — Venice / Naples / Milan

24. Otto Dix — Munich / Dresden / Berlin

25. Francisco Pacheco — Seville / Madrid / Toledo

What are the following doing:

1. Mme Récamier in the portrait by Jacques-Louis David
   (Louvre, Paris)
2. The son in "A Father's Curse" by Jean-Baptiste Greuze (Louvre, Paris)
3. The man in Walter Richard Sickert's "Ennui" (Tate Gallery, London)
4. The passengers in Ford Madox Brown's "The Last of England"
   (City Art Gallery, Birmingham)
5. The angel in Caravaggio's "Rest on the Flight into Egypt"
   (Doria Pamphili Gallery, Rome)
6. The woman in Giorgione's "Tempest" (Accademia, Venice)
7. The Rev. Robert Walker in the painting by Henry Raeburn
   (National Gallery of Scotland, Edinburgh)
8. Georg Gisze in the portrait by Hans Holbein (Gemäldegalerie, Berlin-Dahlem)
9. The Indian Widow in the painting by Joseph Wright of Derby
   (Museum and Art Gallery, Derby)
10. The girls in John Everett Millais's "Autumn Leaves"
    (City Art Gallery, Manchester)
11. The man in Pierre Auguste Renoir's "La Loge" (Courtauld Institute, London)
12. Ajax in Nicolas Poussin's "Realm of Flora" (Gemäldegalerie, Dresden)
13. The young beggar in the painting by Bartolomé Estebán Murillo
    (Louvre, Paris)
14. The central figure in Paul Gauguin's "Where do we come from? Where
    are we? Where are we going?" (Museum of Fine Arts, Boston)
15. Ambroise Vollard in the portrait by Pierre Auguste Renoir
    (Courtauld Institute, London)
16. Belisarius in the painting by Jacques-Louis David
    (Musée des Beaux-Arts, Lille)
17. Nelly O'Brien in the portrait by Joshua Reynolds
    (Wallace Collection, London)
18. The peasants in Jean-François Millet's "The Angelus"
    (Musée d'Orsay, Paris)
19. The young man on the right of Raphael's "Marriage of the Virgin"
    (Brera, Milan)
20. Atalanta in Guido Reni's "Atalanta and Hippomenes"
    (Museo di Capodimonte, Naples)
21. Lady Anne Lennox, Countess of Albermarle in the portrait by Joshua
    Reynolds (National Gallery, London)
22. The boy in John Constable's "Cornfield" (National Gallery, London)
23. Napoleon in Jacques-Louis David's "Coronation of Napoleon"
    (Louvre, Paris)
24. The black boy in Théodore Géricault's "Raft of the Medusa"
    (Louvre, Paris)
25. Giorgione's "Venus" (Gemäldegalerie, Dresden)

In or near which British towns are the following:

Select the correct answer from the three alternatives given

1. The Holburne of Menstrie Museum — Bath / Manchester / Hastings

2. The Ferens Art Gallery — Hull / Leeds / York

3. The Bowes Museum — Bristol / Bradford / Barnard Castle

4. The Burrell Collection — Glasgow / Edinburgh / Aberdeen

5. The Whitworth Art Gallery — Liverpool / Manchester / Burnley

6. The Ashmolean Museum — Oxford / Cambridge / St Andrews

7. The Williamson Art Gallery — Eastbourne / Scarborough / Birkenhead

8. The Walker Art Gallery — Leicester / Leeds / Liverpool

9. The Graves Art Gallery — Sheffield / Newcastle / Brighton

10. Kettle's Yard — London / Cambridge / Bristol

11. The Hunterian Art Gallery — Oxford / Glasgow / Cardiff

12. The Barber Institute of Fine Arts — Birmingham / Norwich / St Albans

13. Temple Newsam House — Swansea / Liverpool / Leeds

14. The Cecil Higgins Art Gallery — Northampton / Bedford / Ipswich

15. The Haworth Art Gallery — Lincoln / Accrington / Birmingham

16. The Laing Art Gallery — Newcastle / Manchester / York

17. The Fitzwilliam Museum — Oxford / Cambridge / Bath

18. The Talbot Rice Arts Centre — Edinburgh / Southampton / Lincoln

19. The Usher Gallery — Sudbury / Chester / Lincoln

20. Sir John Soane's Museum — Edinburgh / London / Bath

21. The Lady Lever Art Gallery — Port Sunlight / Tunbridge Wells / Alnwick

22. The Sainsbury Centre for Visual Arts — Norwich / St Andrews / St Ives

23. Apsley House — York / Norwich / London

24. Christ Church Picture Gallery — Chichester / Cheltenham / Oxford

25. The Shipley Art Gallery — Plymouth / Newlyn / Gateshead

Where are the following located:

1. "The Portinari Altarpiece" by Hugo van der Goes

2. "The Battle of Alexander" by Albrecht Altdorfer

3. "The Laughing Cavalier" by Frans Hals

4. "An Allegory of Venus, Cupid, Folly and Time" by Agnolo Bronzino

5. "Napoleon on the Battlefield at Eylau" by Antoine Gros

6. "The Madonna with Canon van der Paele" by Jan van Eyck

7. "The Hunt in the Forest" by Paolo Uccello

8. "The St Lucy Altarpiece" by Domenico Veneziano

9. "The Three Philosophers" by Giorgione

10. "The Bacchanal of the Andrians" by Titian

11. "The View of Delft" by Jan Vermeer

12. "The Death of Marat" by Jacques-Louis David

13. "The Haywain" by John Constable

14. "The Vision after the Sermon" by Paul Gauguin

15. "The Waterseller of Seville" by Diego Velazquez

16. "The Pearl of Brabant Triptych" by Gerard David

17. "Cardinal Fernando Niño de Guevara" by El Greco

18. "The Flagellation" by Piero della Francesca

19. "The Pietà de Villeneuve-lès-Avignon" by Enguerrand Quarton

20. "The Garden of Earthly Delights" by Hieronymus Bosch

21. "Olympia" by Édouard Manet

22. "The Monk by the Sea" by Caspar David Friedrich

23. "La Grande Jatte" by Georges Seurat

24. "The Feast of the Rose Garlands" by Albrecht Dürer

25. "The Jewish Bride" by Rembrandt

With which groups or movements are the following associated:

1. Maurice Denis, Pierre Bonnard and Édouard Vuillard
2. Franz Pforr, Friedrich Overbeck and Peter Cornelius
3. Charles-François Daubigny, Narcisse-Virgile Diaz de la Peña and Jules Dupré
4. Franz Marc and Wassily Kandinsky
5. William Holman Hunt, John Everett Millais and Dante Gabriel Rossetti
6. Arshile Gorky and Jackson Pollock
7. Salvador Dali and René Magritte
8. Umberto Boccioni, Giacomo Balla and Gino Severini
9. Hans Arp and Marcel Janco
10. Georges Braque, Pablo Picasso and Juan Gris
11. Karel Appel, Corneille (Cornelis van Beverloo) and Asger Jorn
12. Paul Gauguin, Vincent van Gogh and Paul Cézanne
13. George Clausen, Wilson Steer and Stanhope Forbes
14. Harold Gilman, Spencer Gore and Augustus John
15. Ernst Ludwig Kirchner, Karl Schmidt-Rottluff and Erich Heckel
16. Andy Warhol and Roy Lichtenstein
17. Piet Mondrian and Theo van Doesburg
18. Henri Matisse, André Derain and Maurice de Vlaminck
19. Gustave Moreau, Odilon Redon and Pierre Puvis de Chavannes
20. Victor Vasarely and Bridget Riley
21. Claude Monet, Camille Pissarro and Alfred Sisley
22. Agnolo Bronzino, Pontormo and Parmigianino
23. Eugène Delacroix and Théodore Géricault
24. Jacques-Louis David and Jean-Auguste-Dominique Ingres
25. Georges Seurat, Paul Signac and Henri-Edmond Cross

Select your answers from the following: Fauvism - Pop Art - Surrealism - The Nabis - Dada
The Nazarenes - Cubism - Neo-Impressionism - Mannerism - The Post-Impressionists
Symbolism - Romanticism - Der blaue Reiter (The blue Rider) - The Pre-Raphaelites
Impressionism - The Barbizon School - Die Brücke (The Bridge) - Neo-Classicism
The New English Art Club - The Camden Town Group - Op Art - De Stijl - Futurism
Abstract Expressionism - CoBrA

In which town were the following British painters born:

Select the correct town from the three given

1. Frank Brangwyn — Nottingham / Bruges / Hastings
2. William Quiller Orchardson — Edinburgh / Glasgow / Dunfermline
3. Henry Tonks — Solihull / St Albans / Sudbury
4. George Stubbs — Derby / Liverpool / Sheffield
5. Ford Madox Brown — Rye / Winchelsea / Calais
6. Thomas Lawrence — Bristol / Exeter / Bath
7. John Sell Cotman — Ipswich / Norwich / Boston
8. William Clarkson Stanfield — Newcastle / Sunderland / Great Yarmouth
9. John Opie — St Ives / Newlyn / Truro
10. William Etty — London / York / Rome
11. Edward Coley Burne-Jones — London / Florence / Birmingham
12. Edward John Poynter — Rome / Paris / Madrid
13. Benjamin Robert Haydon — York / Plymouth / London
14. Henry Raeburn — Edinburgh / Dundee / Aberdeen
15. David Wilkie — Elgin / Arbroath / Cults
16. William James Muller — Bristol / Munich / Wrexham
17. David Cox — Rhyl / Oldham / Deritend
18. Francis Towne — Exeter / Geneva / Peterborough
19. Walter Crane — Manchester / Liverpool / Leeds
20. John Everett Millais — London / Paris / Southampton
21. Daniel Maclise — Dublin / Belfast / Cork
22. Francis Hayman — Exeter / Bristol / Bath
23. Arthur Devis — Margate / Preston / Gateshead
24. Peter de Wint — Norwich / Stone / Lincoln
25. John Constable — East Bergholt / Flatford / Dedham

In which year did the following die:

Choose the correct answer from the three dates given

1. Masaccio   1428 : 1418 : 1438

2. Raphael   1520 : 1530 : 1540

3. Leonardo   1510 : 1530 : 1519

4. Michelangelo   1564 : 1550 : 1536

5. Giorgione   1500 : 1520 : 1510

6. Giovanni Bellini   1499 : 1505 : 1516

7. Titian   1548 : 1576 : 1590

8. Jacopo Tintoretto   1584 : 1604 : 1594

9. Paolo Veronese   1588 : 1560 : 1600

10. Caravaggio   1600 : 1610 : 1620

11. Peter Paul Rubens   1640 : 1650 : 1660

12. Rembrandt   1639 : 1669 : 1649

13. Jan Vermeer   1675 : 1650 : 1665

14. Anthony van Dyck   1661 : 1681 : 1641

15. Nicolas Poussin   1645 : 1685 : 1665

16. François Boucher   1770 : 1760 : 1790

17. Antoine Watteau   1741 : 1761 : 1721

18. Jean-Honoré Fragonard   1786 : 1806 : 1796

19. Jacques-Louis David   1820 : 1825 : 1830

20. Eugène Delacroix   1863 : 1853 : 1873

21 Théodore Géricault   1834 : 1824 : 1814

22. Jean-Auguste-Dominique Ingres   1857 : 1860 : 1867

23. Thomas Gainsborough   1768 : 1778 : 1788

24. Joshua Reynolds   1792 : 1795 : 1800

25. John Constable   1830 : 1837 : 1835

Where are the following located:

1. "The Martyrdom of St Sebastian" by Antonio Pollaiuolo

2. "The Blinding of Samson" by Rembrandt

3. "The Fall of Icarus" by Pieter Bruegel the Elder

4. "L'Enseigne de Gersaint" by Antoine Watteau

5. "The Diptych of Martin van Nieuwenhove" by Hans Memlinc

6. "The Concert Champêtre" by Titian (or Giorgione)

7. "The Kingdom of Flora" by Nicolas Poussin

8. "The Madonna of the Long Neck" by Parmigianino

9. "The Rest on the Flight into Egypt" by Philipp Otto Runge

10. "The Intervention of the Sabine Women" by Jacques-Louis David

11. "Bathers at Asnières" by Georges Seurat

12. "St Erasmus and St Maurice" by Matthias Grünewald

13. "Jupiter and Io" by Antonio Correggio

14. "The Rape of the Daughters of Leucippus" by Peter Paul Rubens

15. "The Madonna and Chancellor Rolin" by Jan van Eyck

16. "Bonjour, Monsieur Courbet!" by Gustave Courbet

17. "Wivenhoe Park, Essex" by John Constable

18. "Pallas and the Centaur" by Botticelli

19. "Boy with a Club Foot" by José Ribera

20. "The Justice of Emperor Otto" by Dieric Bouts

21. "The Parable of the Blind" by Pieter Bruegel the Elder

22. "The Family of Charles IV" by Francisco Goya

23. "The Virgin of the Rosebush" by Stephan Lochner

24. "The Miraculous Draught of Fishes" by Konrad Witz

25. "The Entombment" by Caravaggio

With which towns are the following most closely associated:

Some of the answers are true, some false - do you know which?

1.	Aelbert Cuyp	Dordrecht
2.	Andrea Sacchi	Rome
3.	Franz von Lenbach	Berlin
4.	Federico Barocci	Urbino
5.	Bernardo Luini	Florence
6.	Hans Burgkmair	Augsburg
7.	Giorgio Morandi	Bologna
8.	Jan Mostaert	Haarlem
9.	Jacopo Tintoretto	Milan
10.	Georges de la Tour	Lunéville
11.	Luca Cambiaso	Genoa
12.	Luis Morales	Badajoz
13.	Sassetta	Siena
14.	Joos van Cleve	Rotterdam
15.	Pompeo Batoni	Naples
16.	Francesco Guardi	Venice
17.	Hans Pleydenwurff	Nuremberg
18.	Bartolomé Estebán Murillo	Seville
19.	Barent van Orley	Brussels
20.	Master Bertram	Dortmund
21.	Vincenzo Catena	Venice
22.	Lawrence Stephen Lowry	Salford
23.	Jacques Daret	Tournai
24.	Adolf Menzel	Berlin
25.	Claudio Coello	Barcelona

Who painted:

			True	False
1.	"The Stonemason's Yard"	John Constable	❑	❑
2.	"Primavera"	Botticelli	❑	❑
3.	"The Oath of the Horatii"	Jacques-Louis David	❑	❑
4.	"The Anatomy Lesson of Dr Tulp"	Rembrandt	❑	❑
5.	"The Death of Wolfe at Quebec"	Winslow Homer	❑	❑
6.	"The Third of May 1808"	Francisco Goya	❑	❑
7.	"Nude descending a Staircase"	Marcel Duchamp	❑	❑
8.	"The Raft of the Medusa"	Eugène Delacroix	❑	❑
9.	"Les Demoiselles d'Avignon"	Edgar Degas	❑	❑
10.	"The Tetschen Altarpiece"	Caspar David Friedrich	❑	❑
11.	"Le Déjeuner sur l'Herbe"	Gustave Courbet	❑	❑
12.	"The Massacre at Chios"	Eugène Delacroix	❑	❑
13.	"The Isenheim Altarpiece"	Matthias Grünewald	❑	❑
14.	"The Burial of Count Orgaz"	El Greco	❑	❑
15.	"The Ambassadors"	Hans Holbein the Younger	❑	❑
16.	"The Scream"	Edvard Munch	❑	❑
17.	"The Tempest"	Joseph Mallord William Turner	❑	❑
18.	"The Funeral at Ornans"	Gustave Courbet	❑	❑
19.	"The Rake's Progress"	Joshua Reynolds	❑	❑
20.	"The Absinthe Drinkers"	Edgar Degas	❑	❑
21.	"The Tribuna of the Uffizi"	Johann Zoffany	❑	❑
22.	"Who's afraid of Red,Yellow and Blue"	Barnett Newman	❑	❑
23.	"The Resurrection: Cookham"	John Constable	❑	❑
24.	"The Hunters in the Snow"	Pieter Bruegel the Elder	❑	❑
25.	"The Mérode Altarpiece"	Hans Memlinc	❑	❑

What nationality are or were the following:

The answers have been mixed up - can you match them correctly?

1.	James Ensor	Scottish
2.	Paul Klee	Irish
3.	Arshile Gorky	Croatian
4.	Daniel Maclise	Austrian
5.	El Greco	Spanish
6.	Richard Wilson	Australian
7.	Giulio Clovio	Swiss
8.	Fernando Botero	Mexican
9.	William Dyce	Welsh
10.	Johan Christian Clausen Dahl	Swiss
11.	Henry Fuseli	Norwegian
12.	Oskar Kokoschka	Armenian
13.	Diego Rivera	Colombian
14.	Sidney Nolan	Belgian
15.	Edvard Munch	Swiss
16.	Juan Gris	Italian
17.	René Magritte	Norwegian
18.	Yves Klein	Cretan
19.	Joseph Beuys	Dutch
20.	Vincent van Gogh	Belgian
21.	Giorgio de Chirico	German
22.	Giovanni Segantini	Danish
23.	Jan Matejko	Austrian
24.	Christen Købke	Polish
25.	Anton Romako	French

What were the first names of the following painters:

1. Sisley
2. Bacon
3. Morisot
4. Arp
5. Géricault
6. Rubens
7. Liebermann
8. Dürer
9. Mantegna
10. Hogarth
11. Fragonard
12. Hobbema
13. Monet
14. Chardin
15. Goya
16. Jordaens
17. Van der Weyden
18. Ingres
19. Daumier
20. Beckmann
21. Corinth
22. Manet
23. Dali
24. Alma-Tadema
25. Redon

Select your answers from the following:-

Berthe - William - Édouard - Alfred - Honoré - Odilon - Salvador - Peter Paul - Francis
Meindert - Jacob - Jean-Auguste-Dominique - Lovis - Albrecht - Jean-Baptiste-Siméon
Andrea - Théodore - Jean-Honoré - Hans (Jean) - Claude - Francisco - Max - Lawrence
Max - Rogier

Who painted the following portraits:

1. "Mr and Mrs Andrews" (National Gallery, London)

2. "Sir Brooke Boothby" (Tate Gallery, London)

3. "Oswolt Krell" (Alte Pinakothek, Munich)

4. "Doge Leonardo Loredan" (National Gallery, London)

5. "The Infante Philip Prosper" (Kunsthistorisches Museum, Vienna)

6. "Duke Federigo da Montefeltro and his Son" (Palazzo Ducale, Urbino)

7. "Ginevra de' Benci" (National Gallery of Art, Washington DC)

8. "Helène Fourment with two of her Children" (Louvre, Paris)

9. "Georg Gisze" (Staatliche Museen, Berlin-Dahlem)

10. "François Marius Granet" (Musée Granet, Aix-en-Provence)

11. "Jean-Jacques Rousseau" (National Gallery of Scotland, Edinburgh)

12. "Jan Six" (Six Collection, Amsterdam)

13. "The Duchess of Alba" (Duke of Alba Collection, Madrid)

14. "Mme de Pompadour" (National Gallery of Scotland, Edinburgh)

15. "Baldassare Castiglione" (Louvre, Paris)

16. "Lord Heathfield, Governor of Gibraltar" (National Gallery, London)

17. "The Bellelli Family" (Musée d'Orsay, Paris)

18. "L'Arlésienne [Madame Ginoux]" (Metropolitan Museum of Art, New York)

19. "Sultan Mehmet II" (National Gallery, London)

20. "La Fornarina" (Galleria Nazionale, Rome)

21. "Francesco d'Este" (Metropolitan Museum of Art, New York)

22. "Anne of Cleves" (Louvre, Paris)

23. "Eleonora da Toledo and her Son" (Uffizi, Florence)

24. "Princess Lieven" (Tate Gallery, London)

25. "Mrs Richard Brinsley Sheridan" (National Gallery of Art, Washington DC)

In which towns are the following:

The answers have been mixed up - can you match them correctly?

1. The Frans Hals Museum — Bayonne
2. The Folkwang Museum — Otterloo
3. The Von der Heydt Museum — Venice
4. The Petit Palais — Chantilly
5. The Calouste Gulbenkian Foundation — New Haven, Conn.
6. The Doria Pamphili Gallery — Paris
7. The Isabella Stewart Gardner Museum — Cambridge, Mass.
8. The Ambrosiana — Haarlem
9. The Kröller-Müller Museum — Essen
10. The Yale University Art Gallery — Paris
11. The Musée Bonnat — Sarasota, Fla.
12. The Metropolitan Museum of Art — Washington DC
13. The Toulouse-Lautrec Museum — Aachen
14. The Fogg Art Museum — Albi
15. The Musée Condé — Paris
16. The Musée Cognac-Jay — Graz
17. The Suermondt Museum — Wuppertal
18. The Busch-Reisinger Museum — Hartford, Conn.
19. The Cà Rezzonico — Rome
20. The Neue Pinakothek — Lisbon
21. The Landesmuseum Joanneum — Milan
22. The Wadsworth Atheneum — Boston, Mass.
23. The Musée Carnavalet — Munich
24. The Ringling Museum of Art — Cambridge, Mass.
25. The Corcoran Gallery of Art — New York

Who painted:

1. "Sarah Siddons as the Tragic Muse"
2. "Louise O'Murphy"
3. "The Venus of Urbino"
4. "The Fighting Téméraire"
5. "The Holy Family on the Steps"
6. "The Doni Tondo"
7. "The Goldfinch"
8. "The Surrender of Breda"
9. "Premonition of Civil War"
10. "Greece expiring on the Ruins of Missolonghi"
11. "The Morning Walk"
12. "Napoleon visiting the Plague House at Jaffa"
13. "The Honeysuckle Bower"
14. "Christina's World"
15. "The Madonna della Vittoria"
16. "The Castelfranco Madonna"
17. "Saturn devouring his Children"
18. "Le Chapeau de Paille"
19. "La grande Odalisque"
20. "Mr and Mrs Ossie Clark and Percy"
21. "The Angelus"
22. "Washington crossing the Delaware"
23. "Ascanius shooting the Stag of Sylvia"
24. "The Syndics"
25. "The Fifer"

Select your answers from the following:-   Thomas Gainsborough - François Boucher
Antoine Gros - Édouard Manet - Andrea Mantegna - Peter Paul Rubens - Diego Velazquez
Giorgione - Andrew Wyeth - Joshua Reynolds - Jean-Auguste-Dominique Ingres - Titian
Joseph Mallord William Turner - Michelangelo - Claude Lorraine - Eugène Delacroix
Nicolas Poussin - Jean-François Millet - Emanuel Leutze - David Hockney - Rembrandt
Salvador Dali - Carel Fabritius - Peter Paul Rubens - Francisco Goya

Fig. 2 "Old Woman cooking Eggs" by Diego Velazquez
National Gallery of Scotland, Edinburgh

What were the first names of the following painters:

The answers have been mixed up. Can you sort them out?

1.	Kandinsky	François
2.	Boucher	Pablo
3.	Vermeer	Nicolas
4.	Seurat	Wassily
5.	Magritte	Pierre
6.	Cranach	Jan
7.	Picasso	René
8.	Vigée-Lebrun	Mary
9.	Rivera	Juan
10.	Poussin	Diego
11.	Turner	Anthony
12.	Courbet	Georges
13.	Van Dyck	Joseph Mallord William
14.	Uccello	Francisco
15.	Cézanne	Paolo
16.	Altdorfer	Hans
17.	Gainsborough	Paul
18.	Cassatt	Elisabeth
19.	Zurbarán	Thomas
20.	Elsheimer	Albrecht
21.	Memlinc	Arnold
22.	Bonnard	Lucas
23.	Rossetti	Gustave
24.	Gris	Adam
25.	Böcklin	Dante Gabriel

What nationality are or were:

Are the answers true or false? - Tick the box of your choice.

			True	False
1.	Richard Diebenkorn	American	❑	❑
2.	Jean Étienne Liotard	French	❑	❑
3.	Yaacov Agam	Israeli	❑	❑
4.	Paul Delvaux	Belgian	❑	❑
5.	Jean (Hans) Arp	French	❑	❑
6.	Rufino Tamayo	Peruvian	❑	❑
7.	William Dobell	Australian	❑	❑
8.	Ferdinand Georg Waldmüller	German	❑	❑
9.	Josef Albers	Austrian	❑	❑
10.	Ferdinand Hodler	Swiss	❑	❑
11.	Constant Permeke	Belgian	❑	❑
12.	James Barry	Irish	❑	❑
13.	José Clemente Orozco	Argentinian	❑	❑
14.	Ceri Richards	Welsh	❑	❑
15.	John Singer Sargent	American	❑	❑
16.	Karel Appel	Danish	❑	❑
17.	Clyfford Still	American	❑	❑
18.	Pierre Alechinsky	Belgian	❑	❑
19.	James Guthrie	Scottish	❑	❑
20.	William Baziotes	French	❑	❑
21.	Gustave Wappers	Belgian	❑	❑
22.	Evaristo Baschenis	Spanish	❑	❑
23.	Wolf Huber	Austrian	❑	❑
24.	James Abbott McNeill Whistler	Australian	❑	❑
25.	Jens Juel	Danish	❑	❑

In which European towns are:

1. The Brera
2. The Ny Carlsberg Museum
3. The Musée Marmottan
4. The Kunsthistorisches Museum
5. The Museo di Capodimonte
6. The Herzog-Anton-Ulrich Museum
7. The Hermitage
8. The Uffizi
9. The Museum Ludwig
10. The Boymans-van Beuningen Museum
11. The Museum Mayer van den Bergh
12. The Städelsches Kunstinstitut
13. The Alte Pinakothek
14. The Stiftung Oskar Reinhart
15. The Pushkin Museum
16. The Museu Nacional de Arte Antiga
17. The Staatliche Museen Preußischer Kulturbesitz
18. The Groeningemuseum
19. The Mauritshuis
20. The Galleria Nazionale delle Marche
21. The Ca d'Oro
22. The Palazzo Pitti
23. The Wallraf-Richartz Museum
24. The Teylers Museum
25. The Rijksmuseum

In art, what do the following usually symbolize:

1. Coral

2. A book

3. A lute with broken strings

4. A distaff

5. A lighted candle

6. An extinguished candle

7. Fasces

8. A clock

9. A sphere

10. A mirror

11. A bridle

12. An anchor

13. A skull

14. A cube

15. Scales

16. A bubble

17. A rainbow

18. A mask

19. A sceptre

20. Bread

21. Bagpipes

22. A torch

23. Dice

24. Smoke

25. A pearl

When did the following die:

Select the correct date from the three given

1.	Joseph Mallord William Turner	1851:1861:1871
2.	Gustave Courbet	1867:1877:1887
3.	Jean-François Millet	1855:1865:1875
4.	Paul Cézanne	1896:1906:1916
5.	Édouard Manet	1883:1893:1903
6.	Claude Monet	1906:1916:1926
7.	Edgar Degas	1907:1917:1927
8.	Henri de Toulouse-Lautrec	1901:1911:1921
9.	Francisco Goya	1818:1828:1838
10.	Vincent van Gogh	1870:1880:1890
11.	Paul Gauguin	1883:1893:1903
12.	Georges Seurat	1871:1881:1891
13.	Henri Matisse	1944:1954:1964
14.	Georges Braque	1953:1963:1973
15.	Pablo Picasso	1963:1973:1983
16.	Salvador Dali	1969:1979:1989
17.	Paul Klee	1930:1940:1950
18.	Gustav Klimt	1908:1918:1928
19.	Egon Schiele	1918:1928:1938
20.	Max Beckmann	1940:1950:1960
21.	Jackson Pollock	1956:1966:1976
22.	Wassily Kandinsky	1924:1934:1944
23.	Marc Chagall	1965:1975:1985
24.	Oskar Kokoschka	1970:1980:1990
25.	Amedeo Modigliani	1920:1930:1940

Which painter:

1. Was killed by the explosion of the Delft munitions factory in 1654

2. Had a raven who could imitate his voice

3. Died of malaria at Porto Ercole in Tuscany

4. Was deaf and dumb

5. Had only one leg

6. Lived on an exclusive diet of boiled eggs

7. Was said to have been poisoned in Rome by jealous rivals in 1428

8. Was obsessed with the seashore scenes of his childhood

9. Drowned in 1650 trying to retrieve his hat from the Tiber

10. Was raped by Agostino Tassi

11. Died at sea and was buried off Gibraltar

12. Helped to pull down the column in the Place Vendôme in Paris

13. Committed suicide in 1592 by throwing himself out of a window

14. Was made a baron by Charles X of France in 1824

15. Drowned himself in 1692 at the age of seventy-five

16. Was left deaf following an illness in 1792

17. Was 'valet de chambre' to Philip the Good, Duke of Burgundy

18. Served as inspector of the Belvedere in the pontificate of Adrian VI

19. Drowned in 1818 while swimming in the Tiber

20. Himself a monk, eloped with a nun, Lucrezia Buti

21. Died at Verdun in 1916

22. Was unable to consummate his marriage after seeing his wife's pubic hair

23. Died with his wife in the Spanish influenza epidemic of 1918

24. Had among his pall-bearers three dukes, two marquesses and three earls

25. Was forced to petition for bankruptcy in 1656

When were the following painted:

1. "The Martyrdom of St Sebastian" by Antonio Pollaiuolo (National Gallery, London)
2. "Diana resting after her Bath" by François Boucher (Louvre, Paris)
3. "Olympia" by Édouard Manet (Musée d'Orsay, Paris)
4. "Pope Innocent X" by Diego Velazquez (Doria Pamphili Gallery, Rome)
5. "Napoleon crossing the Alps" by Jacques-Louis David (Museum, Versailles)
6. "The Denial of St Peter" by Georges de la Tour (Musée des Beaux-Arts, Nantes)
7. "The Ray" by Jean-Baptiste-Siméon Chardin (Louvre, Paris)
8. "The Calumny of Apelles" by Botticelli (Uffizi, Florence)
9. "The Descent from the Cross" by Pontormo (S. Felicità, Florence)
10. "Parnassus" by Anton Raphael Mengs (Villa Albani, Rome)
11. "An Allegory of Venus, Cupid, Folly and Time" by Agnolo Bronzino (National Gallery, London)
12. "The Rhinoceros" by Pietro Longhi (Ca' Rezzonico, Venice)
13. "Queen Mary Tudor" by Antonio Moro (Prado, Madrid)
14. "The Boy with a Club Foot" by José Ribera (Louvre, Paris)
15. "The Oath of the Horatii" by Jacques-Louis David (Louvre, Paris)
16. "Horse frightened by a Lion" by George Stubbs (Walker Art Gallery, Liverpool)
17. "Charles V" by Jacob Seisenegger (Kunsthistorisches Museum, Vienna)
18. "The Funeral at Ornans" by Gustave Courbet (Musée d'Orsay, Paris)
19. "The Studio of the Painter" by Gustave Courbet (Musée d'Orsay, Paris)
20. "Lord Heathfield" by Joshua Reynolds (National Gallery, London)
21. "Alexander and the Family of Darius" by Paolo Veronese (National Gallery, London)
22. "The Coronation of the Virgin" by Lorenzo Monaco (Uffizi, Florence)
23. "The Angelus" by Jean-François Millet (Musée d'Orsay, Paris)
24. "Le Déjeuner sur l'Herbe" by Édouard Manet (Musée d'Orsay, Paris)
25. "The Feast in the House of Levi" by Paolo Veronese (Accademia, Venice)

Select your answers from the following:-   1573 - 1650 - 1751 - 1761 - 1800 - 1863 - 1850 1532 - 1742 - 1475 - 1770 - 1413 - 1859 - 1788 - 1554 - 1652 - 1865 - 1650 - 1494 - 1728 1545 - 1565 - 1855 - 1784 - 1528

Fig. 3 "The Lomellini Family" by Anthony van Dyck
National Gallery of Scotland, Edinburgh

Section Two

CONNOISSEUR

Who painted:

1. "The Rape of Ganymede" (Kunsthistorisches Museum, Vienna)
2. "The Allegory of Faith" (Metropolitan Museum of Art, New York)
3. "Marcus Curtius leaping into the Gulf" (Royal Albert Memorial Museum, Exeter)
4. "La Gloria" (National Gallery of Scotland, Edinburgh)
5. "The Lacemaker" (Louvre, Paris)
6. "The Angry Swan" (Rijksmuseum, Amsterdam)
7. "Quince, Cabbage, Melon, Cucumber" (Gallery of Fine Arts, San Diego)
8. "La belle Ferronière" (Louvre, Paris)
9. "The Procuress" (Museum of Fine Arts, Boston)
10. "The Barbary Pirate" (Louvre, Paris)
11. "Three Studies at the Base of a Crucifixion" (Tate Gallery, London)
12. "The Derby at Epsom" (Louvre, Paris)
13. "Israel in Egypt" (Guildhall, London)
14. "La Maison du Pendu" (Musée d'Orsay, Paris)
15. "Septimus Severus rebuking Caracalla" (Louvre, Paris)
16. "The Beheading of John the Baptist" (Cathedral, Valletta)
17. "The Sonnet" (Victoria and Albert Museum, London)
18. "An Allegory of Rudolf II" (Kunsthistorisches Museum, Vienna)
19. "The Cyclops" (Kröller-Müller Museum, Otterloo)
20. "Studland Beach" (Tate Gallery, London)
21. "The dead Bird" (Alte Pinakothek, Munich)
22. "Rugby" (Musée d'Art Moderne, Paris)
23. "Lesbia weighing her Sparrow against her Jewels" (National Gallery, London)
24. "The Stonebreaker" (Walker Art Gallery, Liverpool)
25. "Outside the Alehouse Door" (Tate Gallery, London)

When were the following painted:

1. "The Ghent Altarpiece" by Jan (and Hubert?) van Eyck (St-Bavon, Ghent)
2. "The Anatomy Lesson of Dr Tulp" by Rembrandt (Mauritshuis, The Hague)
3. "Rain, Steam and Speed" by Joseph Mallord William Turner (National Gallery, London)
4. The "Equestrian Portrait of Sir John Hawkwood" by Paolo Uccello (Duomo, Florence)
5. "The Laughing Cavalier" by Frans Hals (Wallace Collection, London)
6. "The Miraculous Draught of Fishes" by Konrad Witz (Musée d'Art et d'Histoire, Geneva)
7. "The Island of the Dead" by Arnold Böcklin (Kunstmuseum, Basel)
8. "The Madonna of the Rosebower" by Martin Schongauer (St Martin, Colmar)
9. "The Third of May 1808" by Francisco Goya (Prado, Madrid)
10. "The Shrine of St Ursula" by Hans Memlinc (Hôpital S. Jean, Bruges)
11. "The Leaping Horse" by John Constable (Tate Gallery, London)
12. "The Assumption of the Virgin" by Titian (S. Maria Gloriosa dei Frari, Venice)
13. "The Old Shepherd's Chief Mourner" by Edwin Landseer (Victoria and Albert Museum, London)
14. "The Isenheim Altarpiece" by Matthias Grünewald (Musée d'Unterlinden, Colmar)
15. "The Garden of Earthly Delights" by Hieronymus Bosch (Prado, Madrid)
16. "Arctic Shipwreck" by Caspar David Friedrich (Kunsthalle, Hamburg)
17. "The Madonna of the Harpies" by Andrea del Sarto (Uffizi, Florence)
18. "The Adoration of the Trinity" by Albrecht Dürer (Kunsthistorisches Museum, Vienna)
19. "The Fighting Téméraire" by Joseph Mallord William Turner (National Gallery, London)
20. "The Night Watch" by Rembrandt (Rijksmuseum, Amsterdam)
21. "Euridyce and Aristaeus" by Niccolò dell'Abbate (National Gallery, London)
22. "Sir John Luttrell" by Hans Eworth (Courtauld Institute, London)
23. "The Tower of Babel" by Pieter Bruegel the Elder (Kunsthistorisches Museum, Vienna)
24. "The Rape of the Daughters of Leucippus" by Peter Paul Rubens (Alte Pinakothek, Munich)
25. "Ecce Homo" by Antonello da Messina (Metropolitan Museum of Art, New York)

Select your answers from the following: 1515 : 1436 : 1489 : 1432 : 1824 : 1560 : 1642
1814 : 1632 : 1470 : 1617 : 1563 : 1829 : 1550 : 1517 : 1624 : 1444 : 1844 : 1475 : 1518
1837 : 1511 : 1838 : 1485 : 1880

For what categories of painting are the following best known:

Some of the answers are correct, others are mixed up - can you sort them out?

1.	Emanuel de Witte	Portraits
2.	Jan van der Heyden	Altarpieces
3.	Adriaen Brouwer	Low-life peasant scenes
4.	Jan Wildens	Landscapes and hunting scenes
5.	Juan Sánchez Cótan	Still-lifes
6.	Jean-Étienne Liotard	Breakfast pieces
7.	Christoph Amberger	Portraits
8.	Willem Claesz. Heda	View paintings
9.	Gaspare Vanvitelli	Topographical views
10.	Alessandro Magnasco	Religious paintings and fantastic landscapes
11.	Ludolf Backhuysen	Portraits
12.	Federico Barocci	Church interiors
13.	Nicolas de Staël	Flower pieces
14.	Frans Snyders	Animals, hunting scenes and still-lifes
15.	Evaristo Baschenis	Still-lifes, mostly of musical instruments
16.	Gerrit Berckheyde	Architectural views
17.	Anton Graff	Landscapes
18.	Rachel Ruysch	Abstracts
19.	Samuel Scott	Topographical views
20.	Willem II van de Velde	Marine paintings
21.	Aert van der Neer	Frozen winter landscapes and moonlit scenes
22.	Joachim Patenier	Seascapes
23.	Gerard Terborch	Genre and portrait paintings
24.	Melchior de Hondecoeter	Domestic and exotic birds
25.	Willem Kalf	Still-lifes

Who painted:

1. "The Execution of the Emperor Maximilian" (Städtische Galerie, Mannheim)
2. "The Alba Madonna" (National Gallery, Washington)
3. "Flaming June" (Museo de Arte, Puerto Rico)
4. "The Young Englishman" (Pitti Palace, Florence)
5. "Fata te miti" (National Gallery, Washington)
6. "The Colossus" (Prado, Madrid)
7. "View of Toledo" (Metropolitan Museum of Art, New York)
8. "The Rhinoceros" (Cà Rezzonico, Venice)
9. "The Angry Swan" (Rijksmuseum, Amsterdam)
10. "Cornard Wood" (National Gallery, London)
11. "The Judgment of Cambyses" (Groeningemuseum, Bruges)
12. "Louis XIV and his Family" (Wallace Collection, London)
13. "The Distribution of the Eagles" (Museum, Versailles)
14. "The Absinthe Drinker" (Ny Carlsberg Museum, Copenhagen)
15. "The Execution of Lady Jane Grey" (National Gallery, London)
16. "The Bean Feast" (Kunsthistorisches Museum, Vienna)
17. "Fray Felix Hortensio Paravicino" (Museum of Fine Arts, Boston)
18. "The Madonna of the Harpies" (Uffizi, Florence)
19. "The Hon. Augustus Keppel" (National Maritime Museum, Greenwich)
20. "The Burial of the Sardine" (Academy of San Fernando, Madrid)
21. "The Holy Family on the Steps" (National Gallery, Washington)
22. "The Jewish Cemetery" (Gemäldegalerie, Dresden)
23. "Karl Johann Street, by Night" (Private Collection, Bergen)
24. "The Snake Charmer" (Musée d'Orsay, Paris)
25. "Ennui" (Tate Gallery, London)

Select your answers from the following: Titian - Édouard Manet - Andrea del Sarto
Edvard Munch - Raphael - Thomas Gainsborough - Frederick Leighton - Paul Gauguin
Francisco Goya - Joshua Reynolds - Nicolas Poussin - Walter Richard Sickert - El Greco
Édouard Manet - Pietro Longhi - Jan Asselyn - Henri 'Douanier' Rousseau - Jacob Jordaens
Gerard David - Jacob van Ruisdael - Jacques-Louis David - Paul Delaroche - El Greco
Francisco Goya - Nicolas de Largillière

Where are the following located:

Some of the answers are correct, others are mixed up - can you match them up correctly?

1. "The Maestà" by Duccio   Museo dell'Opera del Duomo, Siena

2. "The Wilton Diptych"   National Museum of Wales, Cardiff

3. "The Death of Adonis" by Sebastiano del Piombo   Hampton Court Palace

4. "The Lincolnshire Ox" by George Stubbs   Walker Art Gallery, Liverpool

5. "The Kleptomaniac" by Théodore Géricault   Musée des Beaux-Arts, Ghent

6. "The White Horse" by John Constable   Alte Pinakothek, Munich

7. "The Rev. Robert Walker Skating" by Henry Raeburn   Uffizi, Florence

8. "The S. Trinità Madonna" by Cimabue   Musée de l'Hôtel-Dieu, Beaune

9. "The Last Judgment" by Rogier van der Weyden   National Gallery, London

10. "Émile Zola" by Édouard Manet   Musée d'Orsay, Paris

11. "Belisarius" by Jacques-Louis David   Musée des Beaux-Arts, Lille

12. "The Artist's Studio" by Jan Vermeer   Kunsthistorisches Museum, Vienna

13. "St Louis of Toulouse" by Simone Martini   Museo di Capodimonte, Naples

14. "The Descent from the Cross" by Peter Paul Rubens   Antwerp Cathedral

15. "The Dead Christ" by Andrea Mantegna   Musée des Beaux-Arts, Dijon

16. "Scenes from the Life of Mary" by Melchior Broederlam   Uffizi, Florence

17. "The Triumphs of Caesar" by Andrea Mantegna   National Gallery, London

18. "Noli me tangere" by Titian   Borghese Gallery, Rome

19. "The Hon. Mrs Graham" by Thomas Gainsborough   Brera, Milan

20. "The Crowning with Thorns" by Hieronymus Bosch   National Gallery, London

21. "The Vision of St Bernard" by Filippino Lippi   National Gallery of Scotland, Edinburgh

22. "The Sacred Allegory" by Giovanni Bellini   Uffizi, Florence

23. "Landscape with the Funeral of Phocion" by Nicolas Poussin   Badia, Florence

24. "Sacred and Profane Love" by Titian   National Gallery of Scotland, Edinburgh

25. "The Paumgärtner Altarpiece" by Albrecht Dürer   Frick Collection, New York

What are the following doing:

1. Joseph in Orazio Gentileschi's "Rest on the Flight into Egypt" (Louvre, Paris)
2. Pallas in Botticelli's "Pallas and the Centaur" (Uffizi, Florence)
3. The maid in the background of Titian's "Venus of Urbino" (Uffizi, Florence)
4. The foremost figures in Pieter Bruegel the Elder's "Parable of the Blind" (Museo di Capodimonte, Naples)
5. The curé in Jean-Honoré Fragonard's "The Swing" (Wallace Collection, London)
6. The Duchess of Villars in the School of Fontainebleau double-portrait of "The Duchesse de Villars and Gabrielle d'Estrées" (Louvre, Paris)
7. The boy in Diego Velazquez's "Old Woman cooking Eggs" (National Gallery of Scotland, Edinburgh)
8. Louise O'Murphy in the painting by François Boucher (Alte Pinakothek, Munich)
9. The surgeon-general in Antoine Gros's "Napoleon on the Battlefield at Eylau" (Louvre, Paris)
10. The peasant in Caravaggio's "Conversion of Saul" (Cerasi Chapel, S. Maria del Popolo, Rome)
11. The woman in the open doorway of Jan Vermeer's "Little Street in Delft" (Rijksmuseum, Amsterdam)
12. Bacchus in Titian's "Bacchus and Ariadne" (National Gallery, London)
13. The little satyrs in Botticelli's "Mars and Venus" (National Gallery, London)
14. The musician in the foreground of Pieter Bruegel the Elder's "Peasant Dance" (Kunsthistorisches Museum, Vienna)
15. Mrs Mounter in the painting by Harold Gilman (Tate Gallery, London)
16. Manet in Henri Fantin-Latour's "Atelier des Batignolles" (Musée d'Orsay, Paris)
17. The angel in Jan van Eyck's "Madonna of Chancellor Rolin" (Louvre, Paris)
18. Marten van Heemskerck in the background of his "Self-Portrait with the Colosseum" (Fitzwilliam Museum, Cambridge)
19. The boy on the right in "The Graham Children" by William Hogarth (Tate Gallery, London)
20. The shepherds in Nicolas Poussin's "Et in Arcadia Ego" (Louvre, Paris)
21. The soldier on the right in Matthias Grünewald's "Mocking of Christ" (Alte Pinakothek, Munich)
22. Michel Musson (seated wearing a top hat) in Edgar Degas's "Cotton Broker's Office in New Orleans" (Musée des Beaux-Arts, Pau)
23. The Doctor in the painting by Luke Fildes (Tate Gallery, London)
24. The mounted Turk in Eugène Delacroix's "Massacre at Chios" (Louvre, Paris)
25. Goya in his "Portrait of the Family of Charles IV" (Prado, Madrid)

In Christian art, what do the following trees and fruits usually symbolize:

1. The fig
2. The apple
3. The cherry
4. The orange
5. The gourd
6. The plane tree
7. The lemon
8. The acacia
9. The grape
10. The olive tree
11. The cypress
12. The pomegranate
13. The willow
14. The bramble
15. The cedar
16. The strawberry
17. Wheat
18. The chestnut
19. The palm
20. The quince
21. The peach
22. The oak
23. The almond
24. The elm
25. Holly

Where were the following born:

Are the answers true or false? Tick the box of your choice

			True	False
1.	Francis Picabia	Paris	❑	❑
2.	Giovanni Battista Cima	Conegliano	❑	❑
3.	Giorgio Vasari	Milan	❑	❑
4.	Mark Rothko	Daugavpils, Latvia	❑	❑
5.	Camille Pissarro	St Thomas, West Indies	❑	❑
6.	Peter Paul Rubens	Siegen, Westphalia	❑	❑
7.	Lucas Cranach the Elder	Kronach, Upper Franconia	❑	❑
8.	Jean Fouquet	Paris	❑	❑
9.	Alfred Sisley	London	❑	❑
10.	Johann Zoffany	Frankfurt am Main	❑	❑
11.	Nicolas de Staël	St Petersburg	❑	❑
12.	Jan Gossaert	Amsterdam	❑	❑
13.	Ferdinand Hodler	Lucerne	❑	❑
14.	Willem de Kooning	Rotterdam	❑	❑
15.	Hans Eworth	Bruges	❑	❑
16.	Jean-Auguste-Dominique Ingres	Montauban	❑	❑
17.	Peter Lely	Soest, Westphalia	❑	❑
18.	John Singer Sargent	Naples	❑	❑
19.	Kasimir Malevich	Moscow	❑	❑
20.	Adam Elsheimer	Frankfurt am Main	❑	❑
21.	Amedeo Modigliani	Leghorn	❑	❑
22.	Wassily Kandinsky	Moscow	❑	❑
23.	Henry Fuseli	Zurich	❑	❑
24.	Franz Marc	Dresden	❑	❑
25.	Gustave Courbet	Ornans	❑	❑

Which painter:

1. Developed the technique of frottage
2. Was engaged to complete the series of frescoes in the Sistine Chapel begun by Perugino and others
3. Was known as the 'Raphael of the Netherlands'
4. Often appended the word 'Kres' to his signature
5. Executed the Coronation Portraits of George III and Queen Charlotte
6. Wrote an influential essay entitled *Nothing is Mean*
7. Was appointed official painter to the Doge of Venice in 1474
8. Was appointed Director of the Gobelins factory in 1663
9. Went suddenly blind in 1743 and died insane
10. Was the leading practitioner of the Danube School
11. Was nicknamed 'Crabbetje' (little crab) because of his deformed hand
12. Was the first European artist to depict the landscapes of the New World
13. Was appointed keeper of the Papal seals by Clement VII in 1531
14. Was known in Italy as 'Gherardo delle Notti'
15. Was erroneously stated by Vasari to have murdered Domenico Veneziano
16. Was expelled from Nuremberg for his extreme Protestantism
17. Executed murals in the Houses of Parliament depicting "The Death of Nelson" and "The Meeting of Wellington and Blücher"
18. Ended his years as a lay brother in the monastery in Loreto
19. Produced a series of 'historical' portraits of Emma, Lady Hamilton
20. Was the father of Raphael
21. Taught Umberto Boccioni and Gino Severini in Rome
22. Was the most prominent member of the Kitchen Sink school
23. Was the first Director of the Academy in Seville
24. Is first recorded at the court of John of Bavaria in the Hague in 1422
25. Took a position as a wine gauger with the Amsterdam customs and excise

Select your answer from the following:- Max Ernst - Antonio Tàpies - Meindert Hobbema Sebastiano del Piombo - Jan Asselyn - Luca Signorelli - El Greco - Barent van Orley Daniel Maclise - Andrea del Castagno - Rosalba Carriera - Lorenzo Lotto - Gentile Bellini Charles Lebrun - George Romney - Albrecht Altdorfer - Jan van Eyck - Barthel Beham Giovanni Santi - Bartolomé Estebán Murillo - John Bratby - Frans Post - Allan Ramsay Gerrit van Honthorst - Giacomo Balla

Who painted the following landscapes:

1. "The Bay of Baiae" (Tate Gallery, London)
2. "The Danube near Regensburg" (Alte Pinakothek, Munich)
3. "The Gulf of Marseilles seen from L'Estaque"
   (Metropolitan Museum of Art, New York)
4. "Walton-on-the-Naze" (City Art Gallery, Birmingham)
5. "The Church at Varangeville" (Barber Institute of Fine Arts, Birmingham)
6. "The Flood at Port-Marly" (Musée d'Orsay, Paris)
7. "Salisbury Cathedral from the Bishop's Garden"
   (Metropolitan Museum of Art, New York)
8. "Nocturne in Blue and Silver: Cremorne Lights" (Tate Gallery, London)
9. "Le Château de Medan" (Burrell Collection, Glasgow)
10. "Mousehold Heath, Norwich" (Tate Gallery, London)
11. "Coastal Scene in Picardy" (Ferens Art Gallery, Hull)
12. "The Magpie on the Gallows" (Hessisches Landesmuseum, Darmstadt)
13. "The Villa by the Sea" (Schack Gallery, Munich)
14. "Le Coup de Soleil" (Louvre, Paris)
15. "Coalbrookdale by Night" (Science Museum, London)
16. "A View of the Luxembourg Gardens" (Louvre, Paris)
17. "The Poringland Oak" (Tate Gallery, London)
18. "The View near Albano" (National Gallery, London)
19. "A Bathing Place, Asnières" (National Gallery, London)
20. "La Grenouillère" (National Museum, Stockholm)
21. "Martinique Landscape" (National Gallery of Scotland, Edinburgh)
22. "The Jetty at Deauville" (Musée d'Orsay, Paris)
23. "The Gardens of the Villa Medici in Rome" (Prado, Madrid)
24. "Red Roofs" (Musée d'Orsay, Paris)
25. "Souvenir of Mortefontaine" (Musée d'Orsay, Paris)

Who painted the following portraits:

1. "The Hon. Mrs Graham" (National Gallery of Scotland, Edinburgh)
2. "Juan de Pareja" (Metropolitan Museum of Art, New York)
3. "Émile Zola" (Musée d'Orsay, Paris)
4. "Omai" (Castle Howard, Yorkshire)
5. "The Grand Inquisitor, Cardinal Fernando Niño de Guevara" (Metropolitan Museum of Art, New York)
6. "Napoleon on his Imperial Throne" (Musée de l'Armée, Paris)
7. "The Family of Charles IV of Spain" (Prado, Madrid)
8. "Cardinal Albergati" (Kunsthistorisches Museum, Vienna)
9. "Dr Paul Gachet" (Musée d'Orsay, Paris)
10. "Caspar David Friedrich in his Studio" (Nationalgalerie, Berlin)
11. "Pope Clement VII" (Museo di Capodimonte, Naples)
12. "Diego Martelli" (National Gallery of Scotland, Edinburgh)
13. "Mme de Verninac" (Louvre, Paris)
14. "Isabel Rawsthorne" (Tate Gallery, London)
15. "Cardinal Richelieu from three angles" (Louvre, Paris)
16. "Frédéric Chopin" (Louvre, Paris)
17. "Francis Bacon" (Tate Gallery, London)
18. "Mme Charpentier and her Children" (Metropolitan Museum of Art, New York)
19. "The Princess Metternich" (National Gallery, London)
20. "Ezra Pound" (Tate Gallery, London)
21. "Christopher Isherwood and Don Bachardy" (Private Collection)
22. "Sir Thomas More" (Frick Collection, New York)
23. "Napoleon in his Study" (National Gallery, Washington)
24. "Somerset Maugham" (Tate Gallery, London)
25. "M. Louis-François Bertin" (Louvre, Paris)

For what categories of painting are the following best known:

1. Franz Xaver Winterhalter

2. Bernardo Bellotto

3. Philips Koninck

4. Pierre Soulages

5. Karl Theodor von Piloty

6. Frans Hals

7. Jean-Baptiste Oudry

8. Arthur Devis

9. Simon de Vlieger

10. Luis Eugenio Meléndez

11. Jan van Huysum

12. Martin Archer Shee

13. Antonio Moro

14. Giuseppe Arcimboldo

15. George Knapton

16. Pieter Saenredam

17. Pieter Aertsen

18. William Clarkson Stanfield

19. Andrea Pozzo

20. Pierre-Henri de Valenciennes

21. Giovanni Pannini

22. Pompeo Batoni

23. Nicolaes Berchem

24. Sofonisba Anguisciola

25. Carl Schuch

What are the following doing:

1. The Young Ladies of the Village in the painting by Gustave Courbet
    (Metropolitan Museum of Art, New York)
2. The putto in Nicolas Poussin's "Aurora and Cephalus"
    (National Gallery, London)
3. The central figure in Jacques-Louis David's "Oath of the Horatii"
    (Louvre, Paris)
4. Louis IX in Simone Martini's "St Louis of Toulouse"
    (Museo di Capodimonte, Naples)
5. Christ in Jan van Eyck's "Madonna with Canon van der Paele"
    (Groeningemuseum, Bruges)
6. Thetis in Jean-Auguste-Dominique Ingres's "Jupiter and Thetis"
    (Musée Granet, Aix-en-Provence)
7. Joseph in the right wing of Robert Campin's "Mérode Altarpiece"
    (Metropolitan Museum of Art, New York)
8. The ladies in John Everett Millais's "Hearts are Trumps"
    (Tate Gallery, London)
9. The angels in Andrea Mantegna's "Agony in the Garden"
    (National Gallery, London)
10. The woman on the right in Vincent van Gogh's "Potato Eaters"
    (Rijksmuseum Vincent van Gogh, Amsterdam)
11. The central angel in El Greco's "Burial of Count Orgaz"
    (Santo Tomé, Toledo)
12. The men on the left of "Gersaint's Signboard" by Antoine Watteau
    (Staatliche Museen, Berlin-Dahlem)
13. The woman on the right in Jacob Jordaens's "The King Drinks"
    (Musées Royaux des Beaux-Arts, Brussels)
14. Flora in Botticelli's "Primavera" (Uffizi, Florence)
15. The quack in Jan Steen's "The Doctor's Visit" (Mauritshuis, The Hague)
16. The infant John the Baptist in John Everett Millais's "Christ in the House
    of his Parents" (Tate Gallery, London)
17. Venus in Peter Paul Rubens's "Horrors of War" (Pitti Palace, Florence)
18. The archangel Michael in Rogier van der Weyden's "Last Judgment"
    (Musée de l'Hôtel Dieu, Beaune)
19. Van Gogh in Paul Gauguin's "Portrait of Vincent van Gogh"
    (Rijksmuseum Vincent van Gogh, Amsterdam)
20. Justin of Nassau in Diego Velazquez's "Surrender of Breda"
    (Prado, Madrid)
21. The little girl in Pierre Auguste Renoir's "Les Parapluies"
    (National Gallery, London)
22. The model in "The Artist's Studio" by Jan Vermeer
    (Kunsthistorisches Museum, Vienna)
23. Niccolò da Tolentino in Paolo Uccello's "Rout of San Romano"
    (National Gallery, London)
24. The maid in Titian's "Danaë" (Prado, Madrid)
25. Giovanni Battista Ricciardi in the portrait by Salvator Rosa
    (Metropolitan Museum of Art, New York)

In art, what do the following creatures usually symbolize:

1. The ape

2. The scorpion

3. The butterfly

4. The ermine

5. The hare

6. The toad

7. The camel

8. The rabbit

9. The rat

10. The bat

11. The hedgehog

12. The unicorn

13. The stag

14. The snail

15. The fox

16. The spider

17. The caterpillar

18. The dog

19. The pig

20. The ass

21. The dolphin

22. The centaur

23. The serpent

24. The cat

25. The bee

Who painted:

1. "The Sun of Venice going to Sea" (Tate Gallery, London)
2. "The Two Courtesans" (Correr Museum, Venice)
3. "The Donne Triptych" (National Gallery, London)
4. "The Battle of Lissa" (Österreichische Galerie, Vienna)
5. "The Stud Farm" (Oskar Reinhart Foundation, Winterthur)
6. "The Railway Junction at Bois-Colombes" (City Art Gallery, Leeds)
7. "The Barberini Madonna" (Burrell Collection, Glasgow)
8. "The Skittle Players" (National Gallery, London)
9. "The Punishment of Luxury" (Walker Art Gallery, Liverpool)
10. "Landscape with St George and the Dragon" (Alte Pinakothek, Munich)
11. "Death and the Maiden" (Kunstmuseum, Basel)
12. "The Cannon Shot" (Rijksmuseum, Amsterdam)
13. "Double Nude Portrait: the Artist and his Second Wife" (Tate Gallery, London)
14. "Mushroom" (City Art Gallery, Manchester)
15. "Horses frightened by a Thunderstorm" (Royal Academy, London)
16. "The Swearing of the Oath of Ratification of the Treaty of Münster" (National Gallery, London)
17. "The Cupid Seller" (Museum, Fontainebleau)
18. "The Battle between the 'Kearsarge' and the 'Alabama'" (John G. Johnson Collection, Philadelphia)
19. "São Francisco River and Fort Maurice" (Louvre, Paris)
20. The "Equestrian Portrait of Niccolò da Tolentino" (Duomo, Florence)
21. "The Calling of the Children of Zebedee" (Accademia, Venice)
22. "The Cradle" (Musée d'Orsay, Paris)
23. "The Falconer's Wife" (Musée des Beaux Arts, Caen)
24. "The Poor Fisherman" (Musée d'Orsay, Paris)
25. "Achilles lamenting the Death of Patroclus" (National Gallery of Scotland, Edinburgh)

Which painting:

1. Was badly damaged by suffragettes during an attack at the National Gallery in London on 10 March 1914
2. Is used in their advertisements by its owners, the Scotch Whisky company, John Dewar and Sons
3. Gave its name to the Impressionist movement
4. Was executed by John Constable as a memorial to Sir Joshua Reynolds
5. Gained Jean-Auguste-Dominique Ingres the Grand Prix de Rome on 29 September 1801
6. Was the first picture accessioned by the National Gallery in London
7. Occasioned the legal action brought by James McNeill Whistler against John Ruskin in 1878 after the latter had accused him, in *Fors Clavigera,* of 'flinging a pot of paint in the public's face'
8. Was stolen from the Louvre on 21 August 1911
9. Was the subject of a vituperative attack by Charles Dickens in *Household Words* on 15 June 1850
10. Was purchased by Queen Victoria for a thousand guineas from a picture dealer at the private view of the 1854 Royal Academy exhibition
11. Did Sir George Beaumont frequently carry with him on his travels
12. According to Vasari, 'was carried to the sound of trumpets and amid scenes of great rejoicing in solemn procession from [the artist's] house' through the streets of Florence
13. Was purchased on 6 April 1886 for £2,200 by the soap manufacturers, A & F Pears Ltd, who later used it in their advertisements
14. Was exhibited from 12 June to 30 December 1820 in the Roman Gallery, at the Egyptian Hall, Piccadilly
15. Was destroyed in 1955 or 1956 on the initiative of Lady Churchill
16. Was the first picture at the Royal Academy to require railings to protect it from its admirers since the exhibition of David Wilkie's "Chelsea Pensioners" in 1822
17. Did Joseph Mallord William Turner present to the Royal Academy as his Diploma Piece
18. Was commissioned by Cardinal Giulio de' Medici in competition with Sebastiano del Piombo's "Raising of Lazarus"
19. Resulted from an invitation from the Spanish Government in January 1937 to paint a mural for its pavilion at the International Exhibition in Paris the following summer
20. Completed by Giovanni Bellini, was subsequently altered (notably in the landscape on the left) by Titian
21. First exhibited at the Royal Academy in 1821 as "Landscape: Noon", helped earn its author a gold medal at the Paris Salon in 1824
22. Portrays the company of civic guardsmen commanded by Frans Banning Cock
23. Exhibited at the Royal Academy in 1860, represents the passing of Donati's comet on 5 October 1858
24. Is popularly known in Spain as 'Las Lanzas'
25. Was exhibited at the Royal Academy in 1853 with the title "Our English Coasts 1852"

Which painter:

1. Is famous for his invention of the Eidophusikon in 1781
2. Succeeded Joshua Reynolds as Painter to the King
3. Executed an important series of murals in the Zoological Institute in Naples
4. Was draughtsman to Captain Cook from 1772 to 1775
5. Was the favourite of King Louis-Philippe
6. Began a series of abstracts in 1967 entitled "Ocean Park"
7. Was known as 'Luca fa presto' for the speed at which he produced his prodigious output of paintings
8. Was official painter at Edward VII's coronation in 1902
9. Executed an impressive panorama in 1881 depicting the town and beach at Scheveningen
10. Is sometimes called 'El Esclavo' because he was formerly thought to have been Diego Velazquez's slave
11. Executed the monochrome paintings below Raphael's frescoes in the Stanza della Segnatura
12. Abandoned his frescoes in the Vatican in 1563 because he believed that jealous rivals were attempting to poison him
13. Was described by Émile Zola as 'Impressionism corrected, sweetened and adapted to the taste of the crowd'
14. Shortly before his suicide, executed murals for the ecumenical chapel in Houston, Texas
15. Issued his *Technical Manifesto of Spatialism* in 1947
16. Executed frescoes for Prince Albert at Osborne on the Isle of Wight
17. Earned the nickname 'Andreino degli Impiccati' after painting frescoes on the façade of the Palazzo del Podestà of Florentine traitors hanged by their heels after the battle of Anghiari
18. Journeyed in 1519 via Crete and Cyprus to Jerusalem
19. Submitted a series of pictures of war cripples to the first International Dada Fair in Berlin in 1920
20. Was preoccupied in the 1780's and 1790's with a series of pictures for John Boydell's Shakespeare Gallery and his own Milton Gallery
21. After the 1814 victory over Napoleon, was commissioned to paint a series of portraits of the leaders of the campaign for the Waterloo Chamber at Windsor Castle
22. Was involved in the 1630's in a controversy with Pietro da Cortona as to whether history paintings should be executed with few figures (his opinion) or many (Cortona's)
23. Became a monk in the Convent of San Marco in Florence in 1500
24. Was the leading Macchiaiolo
25. Wrote *The Art of Limning*

In Christian art, what do the following plants and flowers usually symbolize:

1. The violet

2. The columbine

3. The lily

4. The red rose

5. The dandelion

6. The anemone

7. The carnation

8. The poppy

9. The hyacinth

10. Clover

11. The thistle

12. The cockle

13. Jasmine

14. The cyclamen

15. The sunflower

16. Myrtle

17. Hyssop

18. The pansy

19. The white rose

20. Ivy

21. The daisy

22. The narcissus

23. The iris

24. Mistletoe

25. The lily of the valley

Who painted:

1. "Hommage à Eugène Delacroix" (Musée d'Orsay, Paris)
2. "The sick Bacchus" (Borghese Gallery, Rome)
3. "The Great Day of his Wrath" (Tate Gallery, London)
4. "The Lictors returning the Bodies of his Sons to Brutus" (Louvre, Paris)
5. "The Altarpiece of Jacques Floreins" (Louvre, Paris)
6. "The Sistine Madonna" (Gemäldegalerie, Dresden)
7. "La Loge" (Courtauld Institute, London)
8. "The Death of Germanicus" (Institute of Arts, Minneapolis)
9. "Ulysses deriding Polyphemus" (National Gallery, London)
10. "Peter getting out of Nick's Pool" (Walker Art Gallery, Liverpool)
11. "The Monforte Altarpiece" (Staatliche Museen, Berlin-Dahlem)
12. "The Barque of Dante" (Louvre, Paris)
13. "The Diptych of Étienne Chevalier" (Staatliche Museen, Berlin-Dahlem and Musée Royal des Beaux-Arts, Antwerp)
14. "Miravan opening the Tombs of his Ancestors" (Museum and Art Gallery, Derby)
15. "The Fire in the Forest" (Ashmolean Museum, Oxford)
16. "Apparition, Homage to the Square" (Guggenheim Museum, New York)
17. "Chelsea Pensioners reading the Gazette of the Battle of Waterloo" (Apsley House, London)
18. "The Benson Madonna" (National Gallery, Washington)
19. "The Watermelon Eaters" (Alte Pinakothek, Munich)
20. "Autumn Leaves" (City Art Gallery, Manchester)
21. "Gordale Scar, Yorkshire" (Tate Gallery, London)
22. "Suprematism" (Stedelijk Museum, Amsterdam)
23. "Laocoön" (National Gallery of Art, Washington)
24. "The Feast of the Rose Garlands" (Národni Galeri, Prague)
25. "Boat-Haulers of the Volga" (Russian Museum, St Petersburg)

Who wrote:

1. Landscape into Art (1952)

2. From David to Delacroix (1953)

3. Studies in Iconology: Humanistic Themes in the Art of the Renaissance (1962)

4. Classicism and Romanticism and other Studies in the Method of Art History (1966)

5. Meaning in the Visual Arts (1957)

6. On Art and Connoisseurship (1942)

7. Art and the Industrial Revolution (1947)

8. A Century of French Painting 1400-1500 (1949)

9. Artists and their Friends in England 1700-1799 (1928)

10. The Survival of the Pagan Gods (1953)

11. Early Netherlandish Painting: its Origins and Character (1954)

12. The History of Impressionism (1961)

13. Pagan Mysteries in the Renaissance (1958)

14. Florentine Painting and its Social Background (1948)

15. The Social History of Art (1951)

16. Primitivism in Modern Painting (1938)

17. Mannerism and Anti-Mannerism in Italian Painting (1965)

18. Painting in Florence and Siena after the Black Death (1964)

19. Mainstreams of Modern Art (1959)

20. The Portrait in the Renaissance (1967)

21. Academies of Art, past and present (1940)

22. Galleries and Cabinets of Art in Great Britain (1857)

23. Patrons and Painters: a Study in the Relations between Italian Art and Society in the Age of the Baroque (1963)

24. Studies in Seicento Art and Theory (1947)

25. The Birth and Rebirth of Pictorial Space (1957)

What mammals, birds and reptiles are depicted in the following:

1. "St Francis in Ecstasy" by Giovanni Bellini (Frick Collection, New York)

2. "Diana and her Nymphs" by Jan Vermeer (Mauritshuis, The Hague)

3. "A Sunday Afternoon on the Island of La Grande Jatte" by Georges Seurat (Art Institute, Chicago)

4. "In early Spring" by John William Inchbold (Ashmolean Museum, Oxford)

5. "The Madonna of the Meadow" by Giovanni Bellini (National Gallery, London)

6. "The Allegory of Prudence" by Titian (National Gallery, London)

7. "The Madonna with Chancellor Rolin" by Jan van Eyck (Louvre, Paris)

8. "The Nativity" by Piero della Francesca (National Gallery, London)

9. "The Tapestry Weavers" by Diego Velazquez (Prado, Madrid)

10. "The Peasant Wedding" by Pieter Bruegel the Elder (Kunsthistorisches Museum, Vienna)

11. "The Adoration of the Magi" by Botticelli (Uffizi, Florence)

12. "The Long Engagement" by Arthur Hughes (City Art Gallery, Birmingham)

13. "The Portrait of a Young Man" by Jan Mostaert (Walker Art Gallery, Liverpool)

14. "St Jerome in his Study" by Antonello da Messina (National Gallery, London)

15. "The Agony in the Garden" by Andrea Mantegna (National Gallery, London)

16. "The Nativity" by Federico Barocci (Ambrosiana, Milan)

17. "The Satyr and the Peasant" by Jacob Jordaens (Alte Pinakothek, Munich)

18. "St John the Baptist" by Caravaggio (Capitoline Museum, Rome)

19. "An Election: Chairing the Member" by William Hogarth (Sir John Soane's Museum, London)

20. "Rebecca and Eleazar" by Bartolomé Esteban Murillo (Prado, Madrid)

21. "The Young Bull" by Paulus Potter (Mauritshuis, The Hague)

22. "The Three Fates" by Sodoma (Barberini Palace, Rome)

23. "The Baptism of Christ" by Andrea del Verrocchio and Leonardo (Uffizi, Florence)

24. "Olympia" by Édouard Manet (Musée d'Orsay, Paris)

25. "Bacchus and Ariadne" by Titian (National Gallery, London)

In Christian art, what do the following birds usually symbolize:

1. The stork

2. The goldfinch

3. The peacock

4. The cormorant

5. The dove

6. The raven

7. A lone magpie

8. The lark

9. The cockerel

10. The parrot

11. The owl

12. The sparrow

13. The pelican

14. The swallow

15. The woodpecker

16. The crane

17. The partridge

18. The goose

19. The eagle

20. The blackbird

21. The wild falcon

22. The domestic falcon

23. The phoenix

24. The crow

25. The swan

Who painted the following landscapes:

1. "Glencoe" (City Art Gallery, Glasgow)

2. "La Roche percée à Étretat" (Barber Institute of Fine Arts, Birmingham)

3. "Landscape with a Copper Mine" (Uffizi, Florence)

4. "Le Château enchanté"
    (Loyd Collection, on loan to the National Gallery, London)

5. "The Ruins of Brederode Castle" (National Gallery, London)

6. "La Promenade: Memory of the Garden at Etten" (Hermitage, St Petersburg)

7. "Bandits on a rocky Coast" (Metropolitan Museum of Art, New York)

8. "Aurora" (Herzog-Anton-Ulrich Museum, Brunswick)

9. "The Watering Place" (National Gallery, London)

10. "Le Lac d'Annecy" (Courtauld Institute, London)

11. "The Quiet River: The Thames at Chiswick" (Tate Gallery, London)

12. "Heroic Landscape with a Rainbow" (Neue Pinakothek, Munich)

13. "An English Autumn Afternoon, Hampstead" (City Art Gallery, Birmingham)

14. "The Menin Road" (Imperial War Museum, London)

15. "The Magic Apple Tree" (Fitzwilliam Museum, Cambridge)

16. "The Harvest at Montfoucault" (Musée d'Orsay, Paris)

17. "The Terrace at Sainte-Adresse" (Metropolitan Museum of Art, New York)

18. "Landscape with a View of Het Steen" (National Gallery, London)

19. "Dedham Mill" (Victoria and Albert Museum, London)

20. "The large Enclosure near Dresden"
    (Gemäldegalerie Neue Meister, Dresden)

21. "The Falls of Clyde" (National Gallery of Scotland, Edinburgh)

22. "View of Toledo" (Metropolitan Museum of Art, New York)

23. "The Glacier of Rosenlaui" (Tate Gallery, London)

24. "Landscape with a Man killed by a Snake" (National Gallery, London)

25. "La Pie" ["The Magpie"] (Musée d'Orsay, Paris)

Who painted:

1. "Beata Beatrix" (Tate Gallery, London)

2. "The Mystic Nativity" (National Gallery, London)

3. "A Concert in the Tuileries Gardens" (National Gallery, London)

4. "The Madonna del Granduca" (Pitti Palace, Florence)

5. "The Hülsenbeck Children" (Kunsthalle, Hamburg)

6. "Starry Night" (Museum of Modern Art, New York)

7. "The Virgin of the Magnificat" (Uffizi, Florence)

8. "The Gross Clinic" (Jefferson Medical College, Philadelphia)

9. "Madame Moitessier" (National Gallery, London)

10. "Night" (Kunstmuseum, Berne)

11. "The Virgin of the Rocks" (Louvre, Paris)

12. "The Horse Fair" (Metropolitan Museum of Art, New York)

13. "The Emperor Charles V at Mühlberg" (Prado, Madrid)

14. "Totes Meer" (Tate Gallery, London)

15. "Queen Elizabeth I confounding Juno, Minerva and Venus" (Royal Collection)

16. "La belle Jardinière" (Louvre, Paris)

17. "Brook Watson and the Shark" (National Gallery, Washington)

18. "The Virgin of Melun" (Musée des Beaux-Arts, Antwerp)

19. "King Cophetua and the Beggar Maid" (Tate Gallery, London)

20. "La Poudreuse" (National Gallery, London)

21. "The Burial of Atala" (Louvre, Paris)

22. "The Calais Gate" (National Gallery, London)

23. "Le Moulin de la Galette" (Musée d'Orsay, Paris)

24. "The Armoured Train" (Zeisler Collection, New York)

25. "The Madonna della Sedia" (Pitti Palace, Florence)

Who was:

1. Charles Robert Lesley

2. Anne Vallayer-Coster

3. Han van Megeren

4. Giovanna Cenami

5. James Christie

6. Everhard Jabach

7. Gala

8. John Julius Angerstein

9. Marsilio Ficino

10. Jan Six

11. Ambroise Vollard

12. Judith Leyster

13. Gertrude Stein

14. Denis Diderot

15. Peggy Guggenheim

16. Eadward Muybridge

17. Jane Avril

18. Charles Lock Eastlake

19. Marcantonio Raimondi

20. Paul Gachet

21. Francesco Squarcione

22. Alfred Bruyas

23. Giulio Clovio

24. Tom Keating

25. Margaret Lindsay

Of which painter was it said:

1. He achieves a pathos as convincing as nature herself (Théodore Géricault)
2. He could pass for the most 'surrealist' of us all (André Breton)
3. He is the painter of painters (Édouard Manet)
4. There is a man whose qualities can be savoured by people who are getting old (Eugène Delacroix)
5. He seldom painted a picture without considering how Rembrandt or Claude would have treated it (John Burnet)
6. Other painters depict men as they might be; but he depicts them as they are (Annibale Carracci)
7. There is a man who has discovered the tragedy of landscape (David d'Angers)
8. What he did well, no-one did better, and what he did poorly, no-one did worse (Antonio Palomino)
9. His paintings had no semblance of living things but only of antique statues and suchlike things (Giorgio Vasari)
10. He was a good man but did not know how to paint (El Greco)
11. He is a Chinese painter ... lost amid the ruins of Athens (Théophile Sylvestre)
12. He is not a poet, but a historian, for whom the lives of men contain no fairy-tales and no secrets (Herman Grimm)
13. His talent evolved that something new which justifies an artist for his existence (Walter Richard Sickert)
14. He is the only painter of LSD without LSD (Timothy Leary)
15. He made Van Gogh despair (Paul Gauguin)
16. His men and women too often look like wooden figures covered with drapery (William Beckford)
17. He thought it more important to paint light than the objects that are seen by it (Joshua Reynolds)
18. His first efforts were in imitation of Hobbema, but English nature supplied him with better materials of study (Joseph Mallord William Turner)
19. He began by imitating Manet, and Manet ended by imitating him (George Moore)
20 . I knew that one day he would either outstrip us all or go mad in the process: I little realised he would do both (Camille Pissarro)
21. He is second to none amongst the greatest of the old German masters in the arts of drawing and painting (Joachim von Sandrart)
22. He was greater than we thought (Edgar Degas)
23. He did a prodigious number of portraits, about which he took great care at first; but at last he ran them over hastily and painted them very slightly (Roger de Piles)
24. Sometimes when he went back to work he would fall into such a deep thought that he came away at the end of the day without having done anything but think (Giorgio Vasari)
25. I will not admit that a woman can draw so well (Edgar Degas)

Which painter:

1. Was alone in France in openly condemning Napoleon's pillage of art treasures in Italy
2. Was the winner of the first Turner Prize
3. Produced multiple images of Elvis Presley and Marilyn Monroe
4. Was the successor to Joshua Reynolds as President of the Royal Academy
5. Being obliged to spend several hours a day in an earth-closet, felled the fir trees outside in order 'to look at nature'
6. Described Eugène Delacroix's "Massacre at Chios" as 'the massacre of painting'
7. Changed the title of his picture of "The Last Supper" to "The Feast in the House of Levi" after accusations of impropriety by the Inquisition
8. Died in 1642 after falling into a ditch near Haarlem
9. Is famous for his many depictions of the Mont St. Victoire
10. Was instructed by Oliver Cromwell 'not to flatter him at all but remark [his] pimples, warts and everything'
11. Became the City Architect of Regensburg
12. Wrote *ABC de la Peinture* (1921)
13. Was the natural son of Czar Peter the Great
14. Before taking up painting, made designs for Point de Venise lace
15. Entertained the children of the 13th Earl of Derby with his nonsense verse
16. Signed his works with a butterfly motif
17. Provided the frame enabling Eugène Delacroix's "Barque of Dante" to be exhibited at the Paris Salon in 1822
18. Was the only woman (apart from Angelica Kauffmann) to become a founder member of the Royal Academy
19. Concealed his signature in the drapery of his portrait of Sarah Siddons
20. Did Jean-Auguste-Dominique Ingres describe as the future Napoleon of painting
21. Experienced and recorded the visual apparition of a flea
22. Exclaimed to Joshua Reynolds on his deathbed: 'We are all going to heaven and Van Dyck is of the company'
23. Occasionally introduced into his pictures, as a pun on his name, a figure with a gourd bottle at his waist
24. Painted numerous homages to the square
25. Was the owner of a zebu bull, a raccoon and two pet wombats

Under whom did the following train:

1. Rogier van der Weyden

2. Eugène Delacroix

3. Raphael

4. Caravaggio

5. Diego Velazquez

6. Albrecht Dürer

7. Frans Hals

8. Andrea del Sarto

9. Anthony van Dyck

10. François Boucher

11. Leonardo

12. Pieter Bruegel the Elder

13. Hans Holbein the Younger

14. Claude Lorraine

15. Rembrandt

16. Giotto

17. Carel Fabritius

18. Godfrey Kneller

19. Titian

20. Antoine Gros

21. Simone Martini

22. Jacob Jordaens

23. Bartolomé Estebán Murillo

24. Filippino Lippi

25. Joshua Reynolds

What was the relationship between the following painters:

1. Pieter Bruegel the Elder and Jan (Velvet) Bruegel

2. Canaletto and Bernardo Bellotto

3. Augustus John and Gwen John

4. Giovanni Bellini and Andrea Mantegna

5. Hans Holbein the Younger and Ambrosius Holbein

6. Diego Rivera and Frida Kahlo

7. Stanley Spencer and Gilbert Spencer

8. Orazio Gentileschi and Artemisia Gentileschi

9. Robert Delaunay and Sonia Delaunay

10. Frans Hals and Dirck Hals

11. Sebastiano Ricci and Marco Ricci

12. Domenico Ghirlandaio and Ridolfo Ghirlandaio

13. Édouard Manet and Berthe Morisot

14. Filippo Lippi and Filippino Lippi

15. Salomon van Ruysdael and Jacob van Ruisdael

16. Giovanni Battista Tiepolo and Giovanni Domenico Tiepolo

17. Francisco Pacheco and Diego Velazquez

18. Alexander Cozens and John Robert Cozens

19. Jackson Pollock and Lee Krasner

20. Mikhail Larionov and Natalia Goncharova

21. Suzanne Valadon and Maurice Utrillo

22. Taddeo Gaddi and Agnolo Gaddi

23. Arthur Devis and Anthony Devis

24. Otto Modersohn and Paula Modersohn-Becker

25. Francisco Bayeu and Francisco Goya

Fig. 4 "Christ restored to His Parents" by Simone Martini
Walker Art Gallery, Liverpool

Fig. 5　"The Hunt in the Forest" (detail)　by Paolo Uccello
Ashmolean Museum, Oxford

Fig. 6 "An Allegory of Venus, Cupid, Folly and Time" by Agnolo Bronzino
National Gallery, London

Fig. 7 "Hunters Resting" by Aelbert Cuyp
The Barber Institute of Fine Arts, The University of Birmingham

Fig. 8   "Horse frightened by a Lion"   by George Stubbs
Walker Art Gallery, Liverpool

Fig. 9 "Winter Landscape" by Caspar David Friedrich
National Gallery, London

Fig. 10   "Strayed Sheep" by William Holman Hunt
Tate Gallery, London

Fig. 11 "Observation on Shipboard" by Winslow Homer
Collection of Lois Homer Graham

Which saints are commonly depicted in art with the following attributes or symbols of their martyrdom:

1. The keys of Heaven

2. A dish with two female breasts

3. A fish hanging from his crozier

4. A gridiron

5. A spiked wheel

6. A banner with a reed cross

7. A plague spot on his thigh

8. A dish with two eyes

9. A pyx containing the Host

10. A sword piercing her throat

11. An arrow

12. A lance

13. A cup with a snake

14. An anchor tied around his neck

15. A millstone

16. A large saw

17. An organ

18. A cloth bearing the image of Christ's face

19. A stone

20. A tower and a peacock

21. A knife imbedded in his head

22. Three purses or balls of gold

23. A beehive

24. A cloak divided in two

25. An apron full of roses

Where was:

1. Albrecht Dürer from 1520 to 1521

2. Nicolas Poussin from 1640 to 1642

3. Francisco Goya from 1824 to 1828

4. Anthony van Dyck from 1623 to 1627

5. Paul Gauguin from 1901 to 1903

6. Leonardo from 1516 to 1519

7. Peter Paul Rubens from 1604 to 1605

8. Masolino from 1425 to 1427

9. Rembrandt from 1625 to 1631

10. El Greco from 1566 to 1570

11. Jan van Scorel from 1522 to 1524

12. Raphael from 1504 to 1508

13. Jean-Auguste-Dominique Ingres from 1806 to 1820

14. Orazio Gentileschi from 1629 to 1639

15. Vincent van Gogh from 1886 to 1888

16. Diego Velazquez from 1629 to 1631

17. Edvard Munch from 1889 to 1892

18. Caspar David Friedrich from 1794 to 1798

19. Thomas Gainsborough from 1759 to 1774

20. Mattia Preti from 1660 to 1699

21. Jacques-Louis David from 1815 to 1825

22. José Ribera from 1616 until 1652

23. Antoine Gros from 1796 to 1801

24. Hans Holbein the Younger from 1526 to 1528

25. Michelangelo from 1501 to 1505

Who said:

1. A colourist makes his presence known even in a simple charcoal drawing
2. [Of Holbein's "Christ in the Tomb"] This picture could rob many a man of his faith
3. Classicism is health, Romanticism is sickness
4. All art constantly aspires towards the condition of music
5. I don't work *after* nature, but *before* nature - and with her
6. No woman painter knows what style is
7. Painting is its own language, and when you try to talk about it, it's like an inferior translation
8. If people only knew as much about painting as I do, they would never buy my pictures
9. Gros' pictures ... transport me ... into that state of soul which I regard as the most powerful that painting can inspire
10. [Of Ingres] His art is the complete expression of an incomplete intelligence
11. It is difficult to hold the world's interest for more than half an hour at a time
12. I recognise no honour higher than that of having the public as a judge
13. Blake is damned good to steal from
14. Treat nature in terms of the cylinder, the sphere, the cone, all in perspective
15. In Claude's landscape all is lovely, all amiable - all is amenity and repose
16. I try to make concrete that which is abstract
17. A thing well drawn is always adequately painted
18. I am fated to be vilified, and accept it philosophically. But after I am dead they will realise I saw and thought with exactitude
19. Remember that a picture, before being a horse, a nude, or some kind of anecdote, is essentially a flat surface covered with colours assembled in a certain order
20. Painting is for me but another word for feeling
21. There are no schools, only painters
22. Few have been taught to any purpose who have not been their own teachers
23. I paint as a bird sings
24. The sun is God
25. I always start a painting with the sky

In which building are the following frescoes:

1. Pintoricchio's "Scenes from the Life of Aeneas Sylvius Piccolomini"

2. Ambrogio Lorenzetti's "Allegory of Good Government"

3. Masaccio's "Tribute Money"

4. Michelangelo's "Crucifixion of St Peter"

5. Uccello's "Flood"

6. Raphael's "Triumph of Galatea"

7. Piero della Francesca's "Resurrection"

8. Botticelli's "Punishment of Corah"

9. Andrea Mantegna's "Martyrdom of St Christopher"

10. Leonardo's "Last Supper"

11. Masaccio's "Holy Trinity"

12. Raphael's "School of Athens"

13. Fra Angelico's "St Stephen addressing the High Council"

14. Giulio Romano's "Sala dei Giganti"

15. Benozzo Gozzoli's "Journey of the Magi"

16. Giotto's "Dance of Salome"

17. Guercino's "Aurora"

18. Domenichino's "Martyrdom of St Cecilia"

19. Annibale Carracci's "Triumph of Bacchus and Ariadne"

20. Pietro da Cortona's "Allegory of Divine Providence and Barberini Power"

21. Andrea Pozzo's "Allegory of the Missionary Work of the Jesuits"

22. Giovanni Battista Tiepolo's "Marriage of Beatrice and Barbarossa"

23. Agnolo Bronzino's "Crossing of the Red Sea"

24. Simone Martini's "Maestà"

25. Tintoretto's "Road to Calvary"

Section Three

GENIUS

Fig. 12   "The Fortress of Königstein" by Bernardo Bellotto
Manchester City Art Galleries

In what year:

1. Was Peter Paul Rubens knighted by Charles I
2. Was the first exhibition of the Nabis at the Barc de Boutteville Gallery in Paris
3. Was El Greco's altarpiece "El Espolio" commissioned for Toledo Cathedral
4. Was the Antwerp Academy founded
5. Was the Victoria and Albert Museum in London opened
6. Was Egon Schiele arrested and charged with producing indecent drawings
7. Did August Macke and Paul Klee visit Tunis
8. Did Nicolas Poussin leave France for Rome
9. Was Daniel Mytens appointed Court Painter to Charles I
10. Did Gustave Courbet hold his one-man show entitled 'Le Réalisme'
11. Did Rogier van der Weyden paint his portrait of Francesco d'Este
12. Did Dante Gabriel Rossetti, Edward Burne-Jones and William Morris begin their murals in the Oxford Union
13. Was the Salon d'Automne founded in Paris
14. Did Cosimo III de' Medici visit Rembrandt in Amsterdam
15. Did James McNeill Whistler begin painting the Peacock Room in London
16. Did Jacques-Louis David win the Prix de Rome
17. Was Gustave Moreau appointed Professor at the École des Beaux-Arts in Paris
18. Was Elisabeth Vigée-Lebrun summoned to Versailles to paint Marie Antoinette
19. Did Berthe Morisot become a pupil of Édouard Manet
20. Was Simon Vouet appointed Court Painter to Louis XIII
21. Was the Manet Memorial Exhibition in Paris
22. Did Antoine Watteau visit London
23. Was the Society of American Artists founded
24. Did Claude Monet settle in Giverny
25. Was the first Blaue Reiter exhibition in Munich

Who painted:

1. The Sala di Psiche in the Palazzo del Tè in Mantua

2. The "Allegory of Summer" in the Palazzo Rosso in Genoa

3. The Arena Chapel in Padua

4. The Ovetari Chapel in the Eremitani Church in Padua

5. "The Life of St Geneviève" in the Pantheon in Paris

6. The ceiling of the Karlskirche in Vienna

7. "The Last Supper" in the refectory of S. Apollonia in Florence

8. "The Resurrection of the Soldiers" in the Sandham Memorial Chapel at Burghclere

9. "The Expulsion of Heliodorus" in the Stanza d'Eliodoro in the Vatican

10. "The Conversion of St Paul" in the Pauline Chapel of the Vatican

11. "The Miracle at Narni" in the Portinari Chapel of S. Eustorgio in Milan

12. "The Birth of John the Baptist" in S. Maria Novella in Florence

13. "The Assumption of the Virgin" in the dome of Parma Cathedral

14. The Grand Canal façade of the Fondaco dei Tedeschi in Venice

15. The chapel of S. Brizio in Orvieto Cathedral

16. "The Progress of Human Culture" in the Society of Arts in London

17. "The Dream of Constantine" in S. Francesco at Arezzo

18. "Christ giving the Keys to St Peter" in the Sistine Chapel of the Vatican

19. The fresco of "April" in the Palazzo Schifanoia in Ferrara

20. The Camera degli Sposi in the Ducal Palace at Mantua

21. The Chapel and Painted Hall at Chatsworth

22. "The Apotheosis of Hercules" in the Salon d'Hercule at Versailles

23. "The Feast of Herod" in Prato Cathedral

24. "The Allegory of Agriculture" in the Palazzo Medici-Riccardi in Florence

25. "The Annunciation" at the head of the dormitory stairs in S. Marco in Florence

Who commissioned:

1. Botticelli's "Primavera"
2. "The Ghent Altarpiece" by Jan (and Hubert?) van Eyck
3. Titian's "Rape of Europa" in the Isabella Stewart Gardener Museum in Boston
4. Giotto's frescoes in the Arena Chapel in Padua
5. Rogier van der Weyden's "Beaune Altarpiece"
6. Giovanni Battista Tiepolo's frescoes in the Royal Palace in Madrid
7. Paolo Veronese's "Respect, Disillusionment, Conjugal Concord and Unfaithfulness" in the National Gallery, London
8. "The Adoration of the Shepherds" triptych in the Uffizi by Hugo van der Goes
9. Michelangelo's "Last Judgment" fresco in the Sistine Chapel
10. Nicolas Poussin's second series of "Seven Sacraments" in the National Gallery of Scotland, Edinburgh
11. Antonio Correggio's "Danaë" in the Borghese Gallery in Rome
12. El Greco's "Allegory of the Holy League" ("Adoration of the Name of Jesus") in the Escorial
13. Caravaggio's "Death of the Virgin" in the Louvre, Paris
14. Primaticcio's decorations in the Long Gallery at Fontainebleau
15. "La grande Odalisque" by Jean-Auguste-Dominique Ingres
16. Titian's "Bacchus and Ariadne" in the National Gallery, London
17. Annibale Carracci's frescoes in the Farnese Gallery in Rome
18. Diego Velazquez's "Topers" in the Prado, Madrid
19. Raphael's frescoes in the Stanza della Segnatura
20. "The Horrors of War" by Peter Paul Rubens in the Pitti Palace, Florence
21. Masaccio's "Holy Trinity" in S. Maria Novella, Florence
22. Benozzo Gozzoli's frescoes of the "Journey of the Magi" in the Palazzo Medici-Riccardi, Florence
23. Andrea Mantegna's frescoes in the Camera degli Sposi in Mantua
24. Giovanni Bellini's "Feast of the Gods" in the National Gallery in Washington
25. Rembrandt's "Elevation of the Cross" and "Descent from the Cross" in the Alte Pinakothek in Munich

When were the following painted:

1. "The Death of Marat" by Jacques-Louis David
   (Musée Royal des Beaux-Arts, Brussels)
2. "The Laughing Cavalier" by Frans Hals (Wallace Collection, London)
3. "The Burial of Count Orgaz" by El Greco (Santo Tomé, Toledo)
4. "The Battle of Alexander" by Albrecht Altdorfer
   (Alte Pinakothek, Munich)
5. "The Avenue, Middelharnis" by Meindert Hobbema
   (National Gallery, London)
6. "Les Demoiselles d'Avignon" by Pablo Picasso
   (Museum of Modern Art, New York)
7. "The Rucellai Madonna" by Duccio (Uffizi, Florence)
8. "The View of Delft" by Carel Fabritius (National Gallery, London)
9. The "Self-Portrait" by Albrecht Dürer (Prado, Madrid)
10. "Liberty leading the People" by Eugène Delacroix (Louvre, Paris)
11. "The Mystic Nativity" by Botticelli (National Gallery, London)
12. "The Potato-Eaters" by Vincent van Gogh
    (Rijksmuseum Vincent van Gogh, Amsterdam)
13. "The Maids of Honour" ["Las Meninas"] by Diego Velazquez
    (Prado, Madrid)
14. "The Annunciation" by Simone Martini (Uffizi, Florence)
15. "The Ambassadors" by Hans Holbein the Younger
    (National Gallery, London)
16. "The Haywain" by John Constable (National Gallery, London)
17. "The Artist's Mother" by James McNeill Whistler (Musée d'Orsay, Paris)
18. "Giovanni Arnolfini and his Wife" by Jan van Eyck
    (National Gallery, London)
19. "The Transfiguration" by Raphael (Pinacoteca, Vatican)
20. "Disappointed Love" by Francis Danby
    (Victoria and Albert Museum, London)
21. "The San Zaccaria Altarpiece" by Giovanni Bellini (S. Zaccaria, Venice)
22. "The Morning Walk" by Thomas Gainsborough
    (National Gallery, London)
23. "Nude descending a Staircase" by Marcel Duchamp
    (Museum of Art, Philadelphia)
24. "The Adoration of the Magi" by Gentile da Fabriano (Uffizi, Florence)
25. "The Vision after the Sermon" by Paul Gauguin
    (National Gallery of Scotland, Edinburgh)

By what name are the following better known:

1. Jacopo Carucci

2. Giovanni Battista Gaulli

3. Master of the Amsterdam Cabinet

4. Giulio Pippi

5. Gaspar van Wittel

6. 'Il Grechetto'

7. Alfred Otto Wolfgang Schulz

8. Sebastiano Luciano

9. Michelozzo degli Ambrogi

10. Emil Hansen

11. Joos van Wassenhove

12. Andrea di Cione

13. Pietro Berrettini

14. Il Cavaliere Calabrese

15. Michael Lieb

16. Cornelis Cornelisz.

17. Piero de' Franceschi

18. Giovanni di Luteo

19. Balthazar Klossowski de Rola

20. Antonio Pisano

21. Domenico Mecarino

22. Tommaso di Cristofano Fini

23. Domenico di Bartolomeo

24. Jacopo da Ponte

25. Piero di Lorenzo

Who painted:

1. "The Vow of Louis XIII" (Cathedral, Montauban)
2. "Deer in a Forest II" (Kunsthalle, Hamburg)
3. "The Death of Major Piérson" (Tate Gallery, London)
4. "The Dance of Life" (Nasjonalgalleriet, Oslo)
5. "Death on a Pale Horse" (Institute of Arts, Detroit)
6. "The Persistence of Memory" (Museum of Modern Art, New York)
7. "The Blacksmith's Signboard" (Kunsthaus, Zurich)
8. "Luxe, Calme et Volupté" (Collection Mme Signac, Paris)
9. "Dido building Carthage" (National Gallery, London)
10. "Dynamism of a Dog on a Leash" (Albright-Knox Art Gallery, Buffalo)
11. "Windsor Castle in Modern Times" (Royal Collection)
12. "The dead Toreador" (National Gallery, Washington)
13. "The Elephant Celebes" (Tate Gallery, London)
14. "The long Engagement" (City Art Gallery, Birmingham)
15. "I saw the Figure 5 in Gold" (Metropolitan Museum of Art, New York)
16. "The Night Café at Arles" (University Art Gallery, Yale)
17. "Nighthawks" (Art Institute, Chicago)
18. "The Floorscrapers" (Musée d'Orsay, Paris)
19. "Eventide - A Scene in the Westminster Union" (Walker Art Gallery, Liverpool)
20. "The Yellow Christ" (Albright-Knox Art Gallery, Buffalo)
21. "Achille Empéraire" (Musée d'Orsay, Paris)
22. "Three Women in Church" (Kunsthalle, Hamburg)
23. "Le grand Déjeuner" (Museum of Modern Art, New York)
24. "Mère Poussepin" (Barber Institute of Fine Arts, Birmingham)
25. "Cornelis van der Geest" (National Gallery, London)

For which locations were the following originally painted:

1. Peter Paul Rubens's cycle of "The Life of Marie de' Medici" (Louvre, Paris)

2. Paolo Uccello's "Battle of San Romano" series (Louvre, Paris; Uffizi, Florence and National Gallery, London)

3. Matthias Grünewald's "Isenheim Altarpiece" (Musée d'Unterlinden, Colmar)

4. Titian's "Bacchus and Ariadne" (National Gallery, London)

5. Raphael's "Sistine Madonna" (Gemäldegalerie, Dresden)

6. Simone Martini's "Annunciation" (Uffizi, Florence)

7. Duccio's "Ruccellai Madonna" (Uffizi, Florence)

8. Peter Paul Rubens's "Raising of the Cross" (Antwerp Cathedral)

9. Caravaggio's "Death of the Virgin" (Louvre, Paris)

10. Tintoretto's "St Mark freeing a Christian Slave" (Accademia, Venice)

11. Paolo Veronese's "Feast in the House of Levi" (Accademia, Venice)

12. Rembrandt's "Night Watch" (Rijksmuseum, Amsterdam)

13. Diego Velazquez's "Surrender of Breda" (Prado, Madrid)

14. Pieter Bruegel the Elder's "Hunters in the Snow" (Kunsthistorisches Museum, Vienna)

15. Giotto's "Ognissanti Madonna" (Uffizi, Florence)

16. Botticelli's "Birth of Venus" (Uffizi, Florence)

17. Piero della Francesca's "Diptych of Battista Sforza and Federigo da Montefeltro" (Uffizi, Florence)

18. Giovanni Bellini's "Feast of the Gods" (National Gallery of Art, Washington)

19. Andrea Mantegna's "Parnassus" (Louvre, Paris)

20. Albrecht Altdorfer's "Battle of Alexander" (Alte Pinakothek, Munich)

21. Antonio Pollaiuolo's "Martyrdom St Sebastian" (National Gallery, London)

22. Melchior Broederlam's "Scenes from the Life of Mary" (Musée des Beaux-Arts, Dijon)

23. "The Portinari Altarpiece" by Hugo van der Goes (Uffizi, Florence)

24. Fra Angelico's "Deposition" (Museo di San Marco, Florence)

25. Titian's "Presentation of the Virgin" (Accademia, Venice)

Whose self-portraits depict their author as follows:

1. As Holofernes in "Judith with the Head of Holofernes" (Pitti Palace, Florence)
2. With seven Fingers (Stedelijk Museum, Amsterdam)
3. With badges (Tate Gallery, London)
4. As 'a degenerate artist' (Scottish National Gallery of Modern Art, Edinburgh)
5. As Christ as the Man of Sorrows (Alte Pinakothek, Munich)
6. With Dr Arrieta (Institute of Arts, Minneapolis)
7. With a concave view of Delft (National Gallery, London)
8. Holding a painting of a cyclops and satyrs (National Gallery of Ireland, Dublin)
9. In his Oxford University gown with a bust of Michelangelo (Royal Academy, London)
10. With his pug dog (Tate Gallery, London)
11. On a circular Limoges enamel (Louvre, Paris)
12. As if reflected in a convex mirror (Kunsthistorisches Museum, Vienna)
13. With Quappi (Stedelijk Museum, Amsterdam)
14. As Goliath in "David with the Head of Goliath" (Borghese Gallery, Rome)
15. With Franz von Lenbach (Neue Pinakothek, Munich)
16. With a black dog (Petit Palais, Paris)
17. With a view of the Colosseum in Rome (Fitzwilliam Museum, Cambridge)
18. With Fränzi (Kunsthalle, Hamburg)
19. In his museum (Academy of Fine Arts, Pennsylvania)
20. With a self-portrait by Émile Bernard (Rijksmuseum Vincent van Gogh, Amsterdam)
21. As the Apostle Paul (Rijksmuseum, Amsterdam)
22. With a skeleton (Städtische Galerie im Lenbachhaus, Munich)
23. As the shepherd Paris (Wallace Collection, London)
24. As St Luke contemplating Christ's body on the Cross (Prado, Madrid)
25. As a Japanese (Fogg Art Museum, Harvard University, Cambridge, Mass.)

To whom were the following appointed as court painters:

1. Diego Velazquez

2. Jean Clouet

3. Albrecht Dürer

4. Melchior Broederlam

5. Corneille de Lyon

6. Agnolo Bronzino

7. Daniel Mytens

8. Bernardo Bellotto

9. Giuseppe Arcimboldo

10. Hans Holbein the Younger

11. Jan van Eyck

12. Domenico Fetti

13. Sébastien Bourdon

14. Barent van Orley

15. Philippe de Champaigne

16. Anthony van Dyck

17. Lorenzo Costa

18. Jean Baptiste Oudry

19. Adriaen van der Werff

20. Lucas Cranach the Elder

21. Pedro Berruguete

22. Francisco Goya

23. Pierre Paul Prud'hon

24. Sanchez Coello

25. Pieter de Witte

Under whom did the following train:

1. Francisco Zurbarán

2. Frans Snyders

3. Jean-François Millet

4. Luca Signorelli

5. Botticelli

6. Piero della Francesca

7. Andrea Mantegna

8. Pontormo

9. Michelangelo

10. Primaticcio

11. Guido Reni

12. Pietro Perugino

13. Peter Paul Rubens

14. Édouard Manet

15. Piero di Cosimo

16. Francisco Goya

17. Honoré Daumier

18. Gerrit Dou

19. David Teniers the Younger

20. Agnolo Bronzino

21. Nicolas Poussin

22. Giovanni Lanfranco

23. Jean-Baptiste-Siméon Chardin

24. Walter Richard Sickert

25. Allan Ramsay

Fig. 13   "Flatford Mill" by John Constable
Tate Gallery, London

Which painter:

1. Was employed by the Governors of the Netherlands on diplomatic missions to Holland (1627) and Spain (1628)
2. Was ennobled by the Holy Roman Emperor Frederick III
3. Had already established a practice as a portrait draughtsman in crayons at the age of ten
4. Had children christened Rembrandt, Titian, Rubens and Sophonisba
5. Became the first Curator of the Musée Moreau
6. Was the founder of Vorticism
7. Was captured and tortured following the Sack of Rome
8. Drowned in a Venetian canal returning from a Schildersbent party
9. Was Deputy Ranger of Windsor Forest
10. Was imprisoned in 1832 for caricaturing King Louis-Philippe as Gargantua
11. Founded the Norwich Society of Artists in 1803
12. Decided to become an artist after reading Andrea Pozzo's *Perspectiva Pictorum*
13. Is know as the 'Scottish Hogarth'
14. Abandoned painting in 1511 to become an inn keeper
15. Was crippled in a coaching accident in 1819
16. Was made a Count Palatine by Emperor Rudolf II
17. Often painted the figures in landscapes by Meindert Hobbema and Jacob van Ruisdael
18. Grew increasingly blind during the last fourteen years of her life
19. Was the leading figure in the Camden Town Group
20. Was the first director of the Academy of St Luke in Rome
21. Was the leader of the Ashcan School
22. Was appointed Chancellor of the French Royal Academy in 1658
23. Known as the 'Cornish Wonder', was described by Reynolds as 'like Caravaggio, but finer'
24. Received the Order of Merit from George V in 1942
25. Was shot dead by a student in Dresden in 1820

Where was:

1. Frans Post from 1637 to 1644

2. Antonello da Messina from 1475 to 1476

3. Andrea del Sarto from 1518 to 1519

4. Claude Monet from 1860 to 1861

5. Albert Bierstadt from 1853 to 1857

6. Botticelli from 1481 to 1482

7. Giuseppe Arcimboldo from 1562 to 1587

8. Pedro Berruguete in 1477

9. Philipp Otto Runge from 1799 to 1801

10. Piet Mondrian from 1919 to 1938

11. Annibale Carracci from 1595 to 1609

12. Charles Lebrun from 1642 to 1646

13. Marc Chagall from 1941 to 1946

14. Parmigianino from 1527 to 1530

15. Hans Baldung Grien from 1504 to 1507

16. Henri 'Douanier' Rousseau from 1861 to 1867

17. Andrea Pozzo from 1681 to 1702

18. Sebastiano Ricci from 1712 to 1716

19. Arnold Böcklin from 1871 to 1874

20. Camille Pissarro from 1866 to 1869

21. Abraham Bloemaert from 1580 to 1583

22. Max Beckmann from 1947 to 1950

23. Angelica Kauffmann from 1782 to 1807

24. Camille Corot from 1825 to 1828

25. Allan Ramsay from 1738 to 1754

In what year:

1. Did Salvador Dali paint "The Crucifixion" now in Glasgow

2. Was Eugène Delacroix's "Death of Sardanapalus" exhibited at the Paris Salon

3. Was Masaccio admitted to the Florentine Guild

4. Did Claude Lorraine begin his *Liber Veritatis*

5. Did Jackson Pollock have his first one-man show in New York

6. Did Peter Lely become Principal Painter to Charles II

7. Did James Ensor paint his "Entry of Christ into Brussels"

8. Did Uccello go to Venice to work on mosaics in St Mark's

9. Did Benjamin West settle in London

10. Did Joos van Ghent enter the employment of Federigo da Montefeltro in Urbino

11. Did Elias Ashmole found his museum in Oxford

12. Was Gentile Bellini in Constantinople

13. Did Andrea del Sarto go to Fountainebleau

14. Did Pierre Puvis de Chavannes visit America

15. Did Hans Memlinc become a freemason

16. Did Isaac Oliver die in Venice

17. Was Gerard David summoned to decorate the cell of the imprisoned Archduke Maximilian

18. Did Pinturicchio begin decorating the Borgia apartments in the Vatican

19. Did Titian visit the Imperial Court at Augsburg

20. Did Adam Elsheimer settle in Rome

21. Did the Metropolitan Museum of Art in New York open

22. Did Thomas Gainsborough establish his studio in London

23. Did Sánchez Coello become Court Painter to Philip II of Spain

24. Did Fra Filippo Lippi enter the Carmine Monastery in Florence

25. Was the German Expressionist group Die Brücke formed in Dresden

By what names are the following better known:

1. Paolo di Dono

2. Jacopo Robusti

3. Tiziano Vecellio

4. Tommaso di Ser Giovanni di Mone

5. Andrea di Michele di Francesco Cioni

6. Mathis Gothart Nithart

7. Guido di Pietro

8. Michelangelo Merisi

9. Paolo Caliari

10. Christian Emil Maries Küpper

11. Domenikos Theotokopoulos

12. Baccio della Porta

13. Gian-Francesco Barbieri

14. Agnolo Tori di Cosimo di Moriano

15. Domenico Zampieri

16. Jacopo Negretti

17. Orazio Lomi

18. Giorgio da Castelfranco

19. Alessandro di Mariano dei Filipepi

20. Giovanni Antonio Canal

21. Cenni di Pepi

22. Francesco Mazzola

23. Giovanni Antonio Bazzi

24. Domenico Bigordi

25. Antonio Allegri

When were the following painted:

1. "The Raising of the Cross" by Peter Paul Rubens (Cathedral, Antwerp)
2. "The Hunters in the Snow" by Pieter Bruegel the Elder
   (Kunsthistorisches Museum, Vienna)
3. "The Death of Wolfe at Quebec" by Benjamin West
   (National Gallery of Canada, Ottawa)
4. "Madame Récamier" by Jacques-Louis David (Louvre, Paris)
5. "Snowstorm: Hannibal and his Army crossing the Alps" by Joseph
   Mallord William Turner (Tate Gallery, London)
6. "Broadway Boogie-Woogie" by Piet Mondrian
   (Museum of Modern Art, New York)
7. "The Feast in the House of Levi" by Paolo Veronese
   (Accademia, Venice)
8. "The Raft of the Medusa" by Théodore Géricault (Louvre, Paris)
9. "Christina's World" by Andrew Wyeth (Museum of Modern Art, New York)
10. "Captain Coram" by William Hogarth (Foundling Hospital, London)
11. "The Syndics of the Cloth Guild" by Rembrandt
    (Rijksmuseum, Amsterdam)
12. "La grande Odalisque" by Jean-Auguste-Dominique Ingres
    (Louvre, Paris)
13. "The Massacre at Chios" by Eugène Delacroix (Louvre, Paris)
14. "The Four Apostles" by Albrecht Dürer (Alte Pinakothek, Munich)
15. "The Romans of the Decadence" by Thomas Couture
    (Musée d'Orsay, Paris)
16. "The Stonebreakers" by Gustave Courbet (formerly Gemäldegalerie, Dresden)
17. "The Yellow Christ" by Paul Gauguin (Albright-Knox Art Gallery, Buffalo)
18. "The Monk by the Sea" by Caspar David Friedrich
    (Nationalgalerie, Berlin)
19. "Saturn devouring his Children" by Francisco Goya (Prado, Madrid)
20. "The Embarkation from Cythera" by Antoine Watteau (Louvre, Paris)
21. "Impression: Sunrise" by Claude Monet (Musée Marmottan, Paris)
22. "The Scream" by Edvard Munch (Munch Museet, Oslo)
23. "The Adoration of the Magi" by Leonardo (Uffizi, Florence)
24. "Christ in the House of his Parents" by John Everett Millais
    (Tate Gallery, London)
25. "The Infante Philip Prosper" by Diego Velazquez
    (Kunsthistorisches Museum, Vienna)

Who was described as:

1. The Raphael of landscape painting (Horace Walpole)
2. The English Poussin (Anon)
3. The Fra Angelico of Satanism (Roger Fry)
4. The greatest genius that ever touched landscape (John Constable)
5. The first wild man of modern art (Roger Fry)
6. The greatest colourist since Rubens (John Ruskin)
7. The father, the prince, and the first of all painters (Pierre-Paul Prud'hon)
8. A buffalo in wolf's clothing (Robert Ross)
9. The worst artist in the US (*Life* Magazine)
10. That very model of a major minor master (Erwin Panofsky)
11. The Homer of painting (Joshua Reynolds)
12. Fundamentally philistine - commonplace, conceited, and sentimental (R. H. Wilenski)
13. Only an eye but my God what an eye (Paul Cézanne)
14. Someone who knocked you flat with his arbitrariness (Clement Greenberg)
15. The most celebrated of the virtuosi (The council of the Scuola del Carmine in Venice)
16. The strongest of all the Venetians (Paul Cézanne)
17. The bird of paradise in the farmyard of Dutch painting (Anon)
18. One of those appointed to show the world the hidden stores and beauties of nature (John Constable)
19. The most skilful and most excellent painter of the whole Christian world (Romboudt de Doppere)
20. This master of the monstrous...discoverer of the unconscious (Carl Gustav Jung)
21. The only painter of imaginative pictures, apart from landscape, that England has produced (D. H. Lawrence)
22. A war artist without a war (by himself)
23. The Watteau of Surrealism (Sarane Alexandrian)
24. The softest brush ever to give soul to a panel, life to canvas (Luis de Góngora)
25. The glory, the mirror, the ornament of painters (Lorenzo Valla?)

What was the relationship between the following artists:

1. Pieter Aertsen and Joachim Beuckelaer

2. El Greco and Manuel Theotocopuli

3. Diego Velazquez and Juan Bautista del Mazo

4. Jan Molenaer and Judith Leyster

5. Nicolas Poussin and Gaspar Dughet

6. Anton Mauve and Vincent van Gogh

7. Alessandro Allori and Cristofano Allori

8. Giovanni Antonio Pellegrini and Rosalba Carriera

9. George Morland and James Ward

10. Simone Martini and Lippo Memmi

11. Antonio Zucchi and Angelica Kauffmann

12. Hendrick Avercamp and Barent Avercamp

13. Camille Pissarro and Lucien Pissarro

14. Jan van Goyen and Jan Steen

15. Louis Le Nain and Matthieu Le Nain

16. Lodovico Carracci and Annibale Carracci

17. Jean Clouet and François Clouet

18. John Linnell and Samuel Palmer

19. Ambrogio Lorenzetti and Pietro Lorenzetti

20. Jacob Maris and Matthew Maris

21. Domenico Tintoretto and Marietta Tintoretto

22. Domenico Ghirlandaio and Davide Ghirlandaio

23. Aert van der Neer and Eglon van der Neer

24. Jacopo Bassano and Leandro Bassano

25. Federico Zuccari and Taddeo Zuccari

Who were the models for:

1. John Everett Millais's "Ophelia" (Tate Gallery, London)
2. Rembrandt's "Flora" (National Gallery, London)
3. "L'Absinthe" by Edgar Degas (Musée d'Orsay, Paris)
4. The seated female figure in Édouard Manet's "The Balcony" (Musée d'Orsay, Paris)
5. Dante Gabriel Rossetti's "Astarte Syriaca" (City Art Gallery, Manchester)
6. Gustave Courbet's "The Wounded Man" (Musée d'Orsay, Paris)
7. Ferdinand in John Everett Millais's "Ferdinand lured by Ariel" (Collection The Rt Hon Lord Sheffield)
8. "Le Chapeau de Paille" by Peter Paul Rubens (National Gallery, London)
9. James McNeill Whistler's "Arrangement in Grey and Black, No. 2" (City Art Gallery, Glasgow)
10. "The Brown Boy" by Joshua Reynolds (City Art Galleries, Bradford)
11. The figures in Pierre Auguste Renoir's "La Loge" (Courtauld Institute, London)
12. Claude Monet's "Man with a Parasol" (Kunsthaus, Zurich)
13. Caspar David Friedrich's "Two Men gazing at the Moon" (Gemäldegalerie Neue Meister, Dresden)
14. Merlin in Edward Coley Burne-Jones's "The Beguiling of Merlin" (Lady Lever Art Gallery, Port Sunlight)
15. Henry Wallis's "Chatterton" (Tate Gallery, London)
16. Diego Velazquez's "El Primo" (Prado, Madrid)
17. The woman in the foreground of "The Last of England" by Ford Madox Brown (City Art Gallery, Birmingham)
18. "The Fur Wrap" ["Het Pelsken"] by Peter Paul Rubens (Kunsthistorisches Museum, Vienna)
19. Thomas Gainsborough's "Blue Boy" (Henry E. Huntington Art Gallery, San Marino, California)
20. The man with his head immersed in water in Théodore Géricault's "Raft of the Medusa" (Louvre, Paris)
21. The little girl in Frederick Leighton's "The Music Lesson" (Guildhall Art Gallery, London)
22. Andrew Wyeth's "Christina's World" (Museum of Modern Art, New York)
23. The boy on the left in the foreground of El Greco's "Burial of Count Orgaz" (Santo Tomé,Toledo)
24. Pierre Bonnard's "Nude in the Bath" (Petit Palais, Paris)
25. "La Berceuse" by Vincent van Gogh (Kröller-Müller Museum, Otterloo)

Which painter:

1. According to Carel van Mander, 'afraid that he might come to poverty in his old age, always carried crowns hidden in his clothing'
2. Owned a hideous toothless cat named Valentine
3. Prepared his compositions by making naked figures in wax, which he then clothed with wetted paper or thin cloth and arranged until he was satisfied with their disposition
4. Was described by Edgar Degas as 'the giant of dwarfs'
5. Having cut off his ear, washed it and placed it in an envelope before presenting it at a house of ill-repute
6. Had his nose broken and flattened by Torrigiano de' Torrigiani
7. Traveled to the Low Countries in 1520 to petition Charles V for the reinstatement of his annual allowance of one hundred florins, suspended by the Councillors of Nuremberg following the death of the Emperor Maximilian
8. According to Bellori, 'never changed an outfit until it had fallen into rags ... and ... for many years, morning and evening, used the canvas of a portrait as a tablecloth'
9. Was long referred to as the 'Apelles of Europe'
10. Fathered two natural children in London in addition to the four his wife had borne him in Basel
11. Became so mad that he varnished even his clothing, cape and bonnet
12. When the Emperor Charles V retrieved from the floor the brush which he had dropped, exclaimed: 'Sire, I am not worthy of such a servant'
13. Received his nickname after the pupil remained stuck in the corner of his eye
14. Whose figure drawing was a major weakness, maintained that he sold his landscapes and made a gift of his figures
15. Claimed that he began his career in the French merchant marine by restoring the colour to the rinds of a cargo of Dutch cheeses that had become bleached during the voyage
16. Was appointed, first, Gentleman of the Wardrobe and later Gentleman of the Bedchamber by Philip IV of Spain
17. Allegedly could produce from descriptions alone the exact resemblance of deceased people he had never seen
18. Died in 1682 after falling from scaffolding in the Capuchin Convent in Cadiz and rupturing his intestines
19. Was twice convicted for using insulting language during brawls that occurred while he was raffling his pictures
20. 'Had a circular room built in his house in Antwerp with only a round skylight in the ceiling, similar to the Pantheon in Rome, so as to achieve the same perfectly even light' (Bellori)
21. Is reputed to have been so mean that he even saved used tapers
22. Was invested by the Emperor Charles V with the title of a Count Palatine and the Knighthood of the Golden Spur
23. While working as a bookkeeper at the Crédit Foncier, for no apparent reason beat the manager of his department into unconsciousness with his umbrella
24. Took three years to pay off the five guilders' membership fee due to the Guild of St Luke in Delft following his admittance in 1653
25. Was paid $10,000 for a fifteen-second French television commercial in which he rolled his eyes roguishly and proclaimed, 'I am mad, I am completely mad ... over Lanvin chocolates'

In what year was:

1. Baccio Bandinelli's academy founded in the Vatican

2. The Pre-Raphaelite Brotherhood formed

3. The Salon d'Automne in which the Fauves first exhibited together

4. The first Surrealist exhibition

5. The French Academy of Painting and Sculpture founded in Paris

6. The Munich Secession

7. The Salon des Indépendants first organized

8. The Royal Academy in London established

9. The Salon des Réfusés held in Paris

10. The St Martin's Lane Academy founded in London

11. The Brotherhood of St Luke formed in Vienna

12. The first Salon of the French Royal Academy

13. The Dada movement founded

14. The Atelier Suisse founded in Paris

15. Vasari's academy in Florence established

16. The Academy of St Luke founded in Rome

17. The Armory Show in New York City

18. The Berlin Secession

19. The first Salon organized by the Société des Artistes Français

20. The first manifesto of Futurist painting

21. The Degenerate Art Exhibition organized in Munich

22. The Atelier Julian established in Paris

23. The New English Art Club formed

24. The French Academy in Rome established

25. The Vienna Secession

Which painter:

1. Worked on the Ordnance Survey of the Highlands of Scotland after the 1745 Rebellion
2. Died after falling from scaffolding in the Collegiata in San Gimignano
3. Was captured during the Sack of Rome while working on his painting of "St Jerome" now in the National Gallery in London
4. Was the natural son of Charles Maurice Talleyrand
5. Executed a "Death of the Virgin" to replace Caravaggio's in S. Maria della Scala
6. Founded the Pittura Metafisica movement with Carlo Carrà
7. Was jailed for adultery in 1457
8. Was the first President of the Royal Academy
9. Escaped the guillotine by reversing his first and second names
10. Took a medical degree in Caen in 1676 and afterwards practised as a surgeon in Amsterdam
11. Was the inventor of Orphic Cubism
12. Completed Raphael's "Transfiguration" in the Pinacoteca, Vatican
13. First exhibited at the Royal Academy at the age of twelve and died insane
14. Is alleged to have weakened scaffolding in S. Andrea della Valle in an attempt to kill his rival, Giovanni Lanfranco
15. Appears to have remained a life-long virgin!
16. Brought a lawsuit against Frans Hals for enticing an apprentice from her workshop
17. Died in 1824 following a riding accident
18. Is said to have worked in bed and to have dined wearing yellow silk
19. Hanged himself on the opening day of his first one-man show in Paris in 1930
20. Was responsible for hanging the French Academy Salon exhibitions for over 20 years
21. Undertook secret visits to Spain (1427) and Portugal (1428) on behalf of Philip the Good, Duke of Burgundy
22. Exhibited the first painting bearing the initials PRB
23. Succeeded Giovanni Battista Tiepolo as President of the Venetian Academy in 1758
24. Was christened Anton Raphael
25. Was appointed Censor of Paintings to the Inquisition in 1618

By what names are the following better known:

1. Jan Frans van Bloemen

2. Hieronymus van Aken

3. L'Abate Ciccio

4. Giovanni del Poggio

5. Jure Clovicic

6. Corneille de la Haye

7. Bernardino di Betto

8. Frans van Vriendt

9. Francesco Raibolini

10. Gentile de Nicolo di Giovanni di Massio

11. Pieter de Witte

12. Francesco di Stefano

13. Piero di Giovanni

14. Pietro di Cristoforo Vannucci

15. Pieter van der Faes

16. Buonamico Cristofani

17. Antonio di Jacopo d'Antonio Benci

18. José Victoriano Gonzalez

19. Stefano di Giovanni

20. Giuseppe Cesare

21. Karl Schmidt

22. Lorenzo Sciarpelloni

23. Pieter van Laer

24. Gaspard Dughet

25. Jacomo Negretti

Who wrote:

1. Abregé de la vie des peintres (1699)

2. Le vite de'più eccelenti pittori scultori ed architetti (first edition 1550)

3. Diálogos de la pintura (1633)

4. The Analysis of Beauty (1753)

5. Teutsche Academie der edlen Bau- Bild- und Mahlerey-Künste (1675)

6. Le vite de'pittori, scultori, architetti, ed intagliatori (1642)

7. Entretiens sur les vies et les ouvrages des plus excellens peintres, anciens et modernes (1666-1688)

8. Anecdotes of Painting in England (1765-1771)

9. Le vite de'pittori, scultori, ed architetti moderni (1672)

10. Neun Briefe über Landschaftsmalerei (1831)

11. El museo pictórico y escala óptica (1715-1724)

12. Notizie de'professori del disegno da Cimabue in qua (1681-1728)

13. Manifeste du surréalisme, poisson soluble (1924)

14. De diversis Artibus

15. Vies des premiers peintres du Roi depuis M. Le Brun, jusqu'à présent (1752)

16. Het Leven der Doorluchtighe Nederlandtsche en Hoogduytsche Schilders (1604)

17. Arte de la pintura (1649)

18. An Essay on the Theory of Painting (1715)

19. De Groote Schouburgh (1718-1720)

20. Idea del Tempio della Pittura (1590)

21. Het gulden cabinet vande edel vry schilder const (1661)

22. De la loi du contraste simultane des couleurs (1839)

23. Le maraviglie dell'arte, overo Le vite de gl'illustri pittori veneti, e dello stato (1648)

24. The Anatomy of the Horse (1766)

25. Il libro dell'arte

Fig. 14   "The Rehearsal" by Edgar Degas
Glasgow Museums: The Burrell Collection

THE PICTURE QUIZ

The following questions relate to the eight colour and six black and white reproductions placed at intervals in The Art Quiz Book. With the exception of the Winslow Homer, which is in a private collection in the U.S.A., all the paintings are in British collections open to the general public.

Since art is concerned above all with visual experience, the reproductions have been included to enhance the reader's enjoyment of the quiz, and to provide a refreshing break from the text. Even the very best colour reproduction cannot, of course, do justice to the original work of art, and one of the purposes of The Art Quiz Book is to encourage everyone who uses it to make full use of the facilities and services of the many excellent art galleries throughout the United Kingdom and abroad.

1. To which artist was Orazio Gentileschi principally indebted for the style of "The Rest on the Flight into Egypt" *(Fig. 1 page 8)*
2. In which year did Diego Velazquez paint "Old Woman cooking Eggs" *(Fig. 2 page 26)*
3. In which Italian town was Anthony van Dyck resident when he painted "The Lomellini Family" *(Fig. 3 page 34)*
4. What technique did Simone Martini employ for his painting "Christ restored to His Parents" *(Fig. 4 page 65)*
5. Paolo Uccello's "Hunt in the Forest" *(Fig. 5 page 66)* reveals the application of perspective to which style of painting
6. To whom was Agnolo Bronzino's "An Allegory of Venus, Cupid, Folly and Time" *(Fig. 6 page 67)* presented in 1545 by his patron Cosimo I
7. Who is thought to be represented in Aelbert Cuyp's "Hunters Resting" *(Fig. 7 page 68)*
8. Where did George Stubbs witness the incident that inspired "Horse frightened by a Lion" *(Fig. 8 page 69)*
9. Caspar David Friedrich's "Winter Landscape" *(Fig. 9 page 70)* is now separated from its original companion piece. Where is this now located.
10. Which famous Sussex beauty spot is depicted in William Holman Hunt's "Strayed Sheep" *(Fig. 10 page 71)*
11. On board which Cunard ship, as depicted in "Observation on Shipboard" *(Fig. 11 page 72)*, did Winslow Homer travel to England in March 1881
12. The influence of which eighteenth-century Italian view painter is most evident in Bernardo Bellotto's "Fortress of Königstein" *(Fig. 12 page 78)*
13. By whom was John Constable's "Flatford Mill" *(Fig. 13 page 89)* bequeathed to the nation in 1888
14. Like much of his work, the composition of Edgar Degas's "The Rehearsal" *(Fig. 14 page 103)*, reveals the influence of which relatively recent scientific invention

ANSWERS

Page 9

1 William Frederick Yeames
2 John Everett Millais
3 John Constable
4 William Holman Hunt
5 Ford Madox Brown
6 George William Joy
7 Arthur Hughes
8 Edwin Landseer
9 John Martin
10 Luke Fildes
11 Frederick Leighton
12 Richard Dadd
13 Henry Wallis
14 Nicolas Hilliard
15 Dante Gabriel Rossetti
16 William Powell Frith
17 Joseph Mallord William Turner
18 Frank Bramley
19 Robert Braithwaite Martineau
20 David Wilkie
21 George Frederick Watts
22 William Maw Egley
23 William Holman Hunt
24 Edward Coley Burne-Jones
25 Paul Falconer Poole

Page 10

1 Hubert(?) and Jan van Eyck
2 Giotto
3 Raphael
4 Antoine Watteau
5 Joseph Wright of Derby
6 Thomas Gainsborough
7 Jean-Auguste-Dominique Ingres
8 Eugène Delacroix
9 Andrea Mantegna
10 Thomas Couture
11 Diego Velazquez
12 Pierre Auguste Renoir
13 Gustav Klimt
14 Henry Fuseli (Johann Heinrich Füssli)
15 Paulus Potter
16 William Dyce
17 Marcel Duchamp
18 Jean-François Millet
19 Parmigianino
20 Jean-Honoré Fragonard
21 John Constable
22 Edwin Landseer
23 Vincent van Gogh
24 Duccio di Buoninsegna
25 William Hogarth

Page 11

1 Haarlem
2 Bruges
3 Delft
4 Ghent
5 Brussels
6 Antwerp
7 Nuremberg
8 Regensburg
9 Venice
10 Toledo
11 Madrid
12 Munich
13 Dresden
14 Louvain
15 Utrecht
16 Parma
17 Ferrara
18 Arles
19 Cologne
20 Rome
21 Milan
22 Mantua
23 Venice
24 Dresden
25 Seville

Page 12

1 Reclining on a neo-classical divan
2 Leaving home
3 Smoking a cigar
4 Emigrating to Australia
5 Playing the viol
6 Suckling a child
7 Skating on Duddingston Loch, Edinburgh
8 Opening a letter
9 Keeping a vigil beneath her husband's trophies of war
10 Making a bonfire
11 Looking through opera glasses
12 Falling on his sword
13 Cracking a flea between his thumbnails
14 Picking fruit from a tree
15 Holding a statuette by Aristide Maillol
16 Begging for alms
17 Nursing a dog on her lap
18 Praying in the fields during the potato harvest
19 Breaking a rod of apricot over his right knee
20 Stopping to pick up the golden apples dropped by Hippomenes
21 Tatting
22 Drinking from a stream
23 Crowning the Empress Josephine
24 Waving his shirt to attract the attention of a passing ship
25 Sleeping naked in the open air

Page 13
1 Bath
2 Hull
3 Barnard Castle
4 Glasgow
5 Manchester
6 Oxford
7 Birkenhead
8 Liverpool
9 Sheffield
10 Cambridge
11 Glasgow
12 Birmingham
13 Leeds
14 Bedford
15 Accrington
16 Newcastle upon Tyne
17 Cambridge
18 Edinburgh
19 Lincoln
20 London
21 Port Sunlight
22 Norwich
23 London
24 Oxford
25 Gateshead

Page 14
1 Uffizi, Florence
2 Alte Pinakothek, Munich
3 Wallace Collection, London
4 National Gallery, London
5 Louvre, Paris
6 Groeningemuseum, Bruges
7 Ashmolean Museum, Oxford
8 Uffizi, Florence
9 Kunsthistorisches Museum, Vienna
10 Prado, Madrid
11 Mauritshuis, the Hague
12 Musées Royaux des Beaux-Arts, Brussels
13 National Gallery, London
14 National Gallery of Scotland, Edinburgh
15 Apsley House, London
16 Alte Pinakothek, Munich
17 Metropolitan Museum of Art, New York
18 Galleria Nazionale delle Marche, Urbino
19 Louvre, Paris
20 Prado, Madrid
21 Musée d'Orsay, Paris
22 Nationalgalerie, Galerie der Romantik, Berlin
23 Art Institute, Chicago
24 Národni Galleri, Prague
25 Rijksmuseum, Amsterdam

Page 15
1 The Nabis
2 The Nazarenes
3 The Barbizon School
4 Der blaue Reiter (The blue Rider)
5 The Pre-Raphaelites
6 Abstract Expressionism
7 Surrealism
8 Futurism
9 Dada
10 Cubism
11 CoBrA
12 The Post-Impressionists
13 The New English Art Club
14 The Camden Town Group
15 Die Brücke (The Bridge)
16 Pop Art
17 De Stijl
18 Fauvism
19 Symbolism
20 Op Art
21 Impressionism
22 Mannerism
23 Romanticism
24 Neo-Classicism
25 Neo-Impressionism

Page 16
1 Bruges
2 Edinburgh
3 Solihull
4 Liverpool
5 Calais
6 Bristol
7 Norwich
8 Sunderland
9 Truro
10 York
11 Birmingham
12 Paris
13 Plymouth
14 Edinburgh
15 Cults, Fife
16 Bristol
17 Deritend, Birmingham
18 Exeter
19 Liverpool
20 Southampton
21 Cork
22 Exeter
23 Preston
24 Stone, Staffordshire
25 East Bergholt, Suffolk

Page 17

1. 1428
2. 1520
3. 1519
4. 1564
5. 1510
6. 1516
7. 1576
8. 1594
9. 1588
10. 1610
11. 1640
12. 1669
13. 1675
14. 1641
15. 1665
16. 1770
17. 1721
18. 1806
19. 1825
20. 1863
21. 1824
22. 1867
23. 1788
24. 1792
25. 1837

Page 18

1. National Gallery, London
2. Städelsches Kunstinstitut, Frankfurt
3. Musées Royaux des Beaux-Arts, Brussels
4. Schloß Charlottenburg, Berlin
5. Hôpital St Jean, Bruges
6. Louvre, Paris
7. Gemäldegalerie, Dresden
8. Uffizi, Florence
9. Kunsthalle, Hamburg
10. Louvre, Paris
11. National Gallery, London
12. Alte Pinakothek, Munich
13. Kunsthistorisches Museum, Vienna
14. Alte Pinakothek, Munich
15. Louvre, Paris
16. Musée Fabre, Montpellier
17. National Gallery of Art, Washington DC
18. Uffizi, Florence
19. Louvre, Paris
20. Musées Royaux des Beaux-Arts, Brussels
21. Galeria Nazionale di Capodimonte, Naples
22. Prado, Madrid
23. Wallraf-Richartz-Museum, Cologne
24. Musée d'Art et d'Histoire, Geneva
25. Pinacoteca, Vatican

Page 19

1. Dordrecht
2. Rome
3. Munich
4. Urbino
5. Milan
6. Augsburg
7. Bologna
8. Haarlem
9. Venice
10. Lunéville
11. Genoa
12. Badajoz
13. Siena
14. Antwerp
15. Rome
16. Venice
17. Nuremberg
18. Seville
19. Brussels
20. Hamburg
21. Venice
22. Salford
23. Tournai
24. Berlin
25. Madrid

Page 20

1. Canaletto
2. Botticelli
3. Jacques-Louis David
4. Rembrandt
5. Benjamin West
6. Francisco Goya
7. Marcel Duchamp
8. Théodore Géricault
9. Pablo Picasso
10. Caspar David Friedrich
11. Édouard Manet
12. Eugène Delacroix
13. Matthias Grünewald
14. El Greco
15. Hans Holbein the Younger
16. Edvard Munch
17. Giorgione
18. Gustave Courbet
19. William Hogarth
20. Edgar Degas
21. Johann Zoffany
22. Barnett Newman
23. Stanley Spencer
24. Pieter Bruegel the Elder
25. Robert Campin/The Master of Flémalle

Page 25

1 Joshua Reynolds
2 François Boucher
3 Titian
4 Joseph Mallord William Turner
5 Nicolas Poussin
6 Michelangelo
7 Carel Fabritius
8 Diego Velazquez
9 Salvador Dali
10 Eugène Delacroix
11 Thomas Gainsborough
12 Antoine Gros
13 Peter Paul Rubens
14 Andrew Wyeth
15 Andrea Mantegna
16 Giorgione
17 Francisco Goya
18 Peter Paul Rubens
19 Jean-Auguste-Dominique Ingres
20 David Hockney
21 Jean-François Millet
22 Emanuel Leutze
23 Claude Lorraine
24 Rembrandt
25 Édouard Manet

Page 27

1 Wassily
2 François
3 Jan
4 Georges
5 René
6 Lucas
7 Pablo
8 Elisabeth
9 Diego
10 Nicolas
11 Joseph Mallord William
12 Gustave
13 Anthony
14 Paolo
15 Paul
16 Albrecht
17 Thomas
18 Mary
19 Francisco
20 Adam
21 Hans
22 Pierre
23 Dante Gabriel
24 Juan
25 Arnold

Page 28

1 American
2 Swiss
3 Israeli
4 Belgian
5 French
6 Mexican
7 Australian
8 Austrian
9 German
10 Swiss
11 Belgian
12 Irish
13 Mexican
14 Welsh
15 American
16 Dutch
17 American
18 Belgian
19 Scottish
20 American
21 Belgian
22 Italian
23 Austrian
24 American
25 Danish

Page 29

1 Milan
2 Copenhagen
3 Paris
4 Vienna
5 Naples
6 Brunswick
7 St Petersburg
8 Florence
9 Cologne
10 Rotterdam
11 Antwerp
12 Frankfurt
13 Munich
14 Winterthur
15 Moscow
16 Lisbon
17 Berlin
18 Bruges
19 The Hague
20 Urbino
21 Venice
22 Florence
23 Cologne
24 Haarlem
25 Amsterdam

Page 36

1 Antonio Correggio
2 Jan Vermeer
3 Benjamin Robert Haydon
4 John Phillip
5 Jan Vermeer
6 Jan Asselyn
7 Juan Sánchez Cotán
8 Giovanni Antonio Boltraffio
9 Dirck van Baburen
10 Pier Francesco Mola
11 Francis Bacon
12 Théodore Géricault
13 Edward Poynter
14 Paul Cézanne
15 Jean-Baptiste Greuze
16 Caravaggio
17 William Mulready
18 Bartholomeus Spranger
19 Odilon Redon
20 Vanessa Bell
21 Jacopo de' Barbari
22 André Lhôte
23 Godfried Schalcken
24 John Brett
25 George Morland

Page 37

1 1432
2 1632
3 1844
4 1436
5 1624
6 1444
7 1880
8 1475
9 1814
10 1489
11 1829
12 1518
13 1837
14 1515
15 1485
16 1824
17 1517
18 1511
19 1838
20 1642
21 1560
22 1550
23 1563
24 1617
25 1470

Page 38

1 Church interiors
2 View paintings
3 Low-life peasant scenes
4 Landscapes and hunting scenes
5 Still-lifes
6 Portraits
7 Portraits
8 Breakfast pieces
9 Topographical views
10 Religious paintings and fantastic landscapes
11 Seascapes
12 Altarpieces
13 Abstracts
14 Animals, hunting scenes and still-lifes
15 Still-lifes, mostly of musical instruments
16 Architectural views
17 Portraits
18 Flower pieces
19 Topographical views
20 Marine paintings
21 Frozen winter landscapes and moonlit scenes
22 Landscapes
23 Genre and portrait paintings
24 Domestic and exotic birds
25 Still-lifes

Page 39

1 Édouard Manet
2 Raphael
3 Frederick Leighton
4 Titian
5 Paul Gauguin
6 Francisco Goya
7 El Greco
8 Pietro Longhi
9 Jan Asselyn
10 Thomas Gainsborough
11 Gerard David
12 Nicolas de Largillière
13 Jacques-Louis David
14 Édouard Manet
15 Paul Delaroche
16 Jacob Jordaens
17 El Greco
18 Andrea del Sarto
19 Joshua Reynolds
20 Francisco Goya
21 Nicolas Poussin
22 Jacob van Ruisdael
23 Edvard Munch
24 Henri 'Douanier' Rousseau
25 Walter Richard Sickert

Page 40

1 Museo dell'Opera del Duomo, Siena
2 National Gallery, London
3 Uffizi, Florence
4 Walker Art Gallery, Liverpool
5 Musée des Beaux-Arts, Ghent
6 Frick Collection, New York
7 National Gallery of Scotland, Edinburgh
8 Uffizi, Florence
9 Musée de l'Hôtel-Dieu, Beaune
10 Musée d'Orsay, Paris
11 Musée des Beaux-Arts, Lille
12 Kunsthistorisches Museum, Vienna
13 Museo di Capodimonte, Naples
14 Antwerp Cathedral
15 Brera, Milan
16 Musée des Beaux-Arts, Dijon
17 Hampton Court Palace
18 National Gallery, London
19 National Gallery of Scotland, Edinburgh
20 National Gallery, London
21 Badia, Florence
22 Uffizi, Florence
23 National Museum of Wales, Cardiff
24 Borghese Gallery, Rome
25 Alte Pinakothek, Munich

Page 41

1 Sleeping
2 Pulling the centaur's hair
3 Kneeling in front of a cassone
4 Tumbling into a ditch
5 Spying from bushes on the lady on the swing
6 Holding her companion's right nipple between her finger and thumb
7 Holding a melon
8 Sprawling naked on her stomach on a sofa
9 Attending to the wounded
10 Holding the bridle of Saul's horse
11 Making lace
12 Playing with Mars' armour and lance
13 Leaping from his chariot
14 Playing the bagpipes
15 Sitting at her breakfast table
16 Sitting at his easel
17 Placing a crown on the Virgin's head
18 Sketching the ruins
19 Playing a music box
20 Deciphering the inscription on the tomb
21 Beating Christ with a knotted rope
22 Testing a sample of cotton
23 Keeping a night-time vigil beside a sick child
24 Unsheathing his scimitar and knocking defenseless Greek women to the ground
25 Standing at his easel

Page 42

1 Lust or fertility
2 Evil and the Fall of Man. Held by Christ, it refers to his role as Redeemer
3 The fruit of Paradise. Three represent the blood-stained nails; seven, the sorrows of the Virgin
4 Purity and chastity
5 The Resurrection or redemption
6 The charity of Christ
7 Fidelity in love
8 The immortality of the soul
9 The blood of Christ
10 Peace
11 Death
12 The Resurrection, the chastity of the Virgin, or the unity of the Church
13 The Gospel of Christ
14 The purity of the Virgin
15 Christ
16 Humility and perfect righteousness
17 The bread of the Eucharist
18 Chastity
19 The martyr's victory over death
20 Evil and the Fall of Man
21 Truth
22 The strength of faith and virtue
23 Divine approval or the purity of the Virgin
24 The strength of the devout
25 The passion of Christ

Page 43

1 Paris
2 Conegliano
3 Arezzo
4 Daugavpils, Latvia
5 St Thomas, West Indies
6 Siegen, Westphalia
7 Kronach, Upper Franconia
8 Tours
9 Paris
10 Frankfurt am Main
11 St Petersburg
12 Maubeuge
13 Berne
14 Rotterdam
15 Antwerp
16 Montauban
17 Soest, Westphalia
18 Florence
19 Kiev
20 Frankfurt am Main
21 Leghorn
22 Moscow
23 Zurich
24 Munich
25 Ornans

Page 44

1 Max Ernst
2 Luca Signorelli
3 Barent van Orley
4 El Greco
5 Allan Ramsay
6 Antonio Tàpies
7 Gentile Bellini
8 Charles Lebrun
9 Rosalba Carriera
10 Albrecht Altdorfer
11 Jan Asselyn
12 Frans Post
13 Sebastiano del Piombo
14 Gerrit van Honthorst
15 Andrea del Castagno
16 Barthel Beham
17 Daniel Maclise
18 Lorenzo Lotto
19 George Romney
20 Giovanni Santi
21 Giacomo Balla
22 John Bratby
23 Bartolomé Esteban Murillo
24 Jan van Eyck
25 Meindert Hobbema

Page 45

1 Joseph Mallord William Turner
2 Albrecht Altdorfer
3 Paul Cézanne
4 Ford Madox Brown
5 Claude Monet
6 Afred Sisley
7 John Constable
8 James McNeill Whistler
9 Paul Cézanne
10 John Crome
11 Richard Parkes Bonington
12 Pieter Bruegel the Elder
13 Arnold Böcklin
14 Jacob Ruisdael
15 Philip James de Loutherbourg
16 Jacques-Louis David
17 John Crome
18 Gaspard Poussin
19 Georges Seurat
20 Pierre Auguste Renoir
21 Paul Gauguin
22 Eugène Boudin
23 Diego Velazquez
24 Camille Pissarro
25 Camille Corot

Page 46

1 Thomas Gainsborough
2 Diego Velazquez
3 Édouard Manet
4 Joshua Reynolds
5 El Greco
6 Jean-Auguste-Dominique Ingres
7 Francisco Goya
8 Jan van Eyck
9 Vincent van Gogh
10 Georg Friedrich Kersting
11 Sebastiano del Piombo
12 Edgar Degas
13 Jacques-Louis David
14 Francis Bacon
15 Philippe de Champaigne
16 Eugène Delacroix
17 Lucian Freud
18 Pierre Auguste Renoir
19 Edgar Degas
20 Percy Wyndham Lewis
21 David Hockney
22 Hans Holbein the Younger
23 Jacques-Louis David
24 Graham Sutherland
25 Jean-Auguste-Dominique Ingres

Page 47

1 Portraits
2 View paintings
3 Panoramic landscapes
4 Abstracts
5 Historical subjects
6 Portraits
7 Royal hunts and still-lifes
8 Conversation pieces
9 Seascapes
10 Still-lifes
11 Flower paintings
12 Portraits
13 Portraits
14 Bizarre arrangements of flowers, fruits, vegetables, etc, to resemble human forms
15 Portraits
16 Architectural subjects
17 Still-life and genre subjects
18 Marine and landscape paintings
19 Illusionistic ceilings
20 Landscapes
21 View paintings and capricci
22 Portraits
23 Italianate landscapes
24 Portraits
25 Still-lifes and landscapes

Page 48

1 Giving alms to a young girl cowherd
2 Showing Cephalus a small portrait of his wife Procris
3 Holding up the swords he is about to give to his triplet sons
4 Crowning Robert of Anjou
5 Pinioning the wings of a green parakeet (a symbol of sin)
6 Caressing Jupiter's beard
7 Making mouse-traps
8 Playing dummy whist
9 Holding the instruments of Christ's passion
10 Pouring liquid from a kettle into cups
11 Transporting the Count's soul to heaven
12 Packing (or unpacking) pictures
13 Wiping her child's bottom
14 Strewing flowers from her gathered skirts
15 Testing his patient for pregnancy
16 Bringing a bowl of water to bathe the wound in Christ's hand
17 Endeavouring to restrain Mars (the God of War), in whose train come pestilence and famine
18 Weighing in his scales the souls of the Saved and the Damned
19 Painting a vase of sunflowers outdoors in Arles
20 Presenting the key of the city of Breda to the Spanish commander, Ambrogio Spinola
21 Holding a wooden hoop and stick
22 Posing with a large book and a fine trumpet (both symbols of Fame)
23 Directing the attack of Florentine forces against the Sienese on 1 June 1432
24 Attempting to catch in her apron the shower of gold into which Jupiter has transformed himself
25 Writing on a skull the Greek words 'Behold, Whither, When'

Page 49

1 Lust, sexual promiscuity and heresy
2 Envy and hatred
3 The resurrected soul
4 Chastity and virtue
5 Lust
6 Death
7 Temperance
8 Lust
9 Decay and the passing of time
10 Night
11 Gluttony
12 Female chastity and virginity
13 Piety and religious aspiration or lust
14 Sloth
15 Cunning and guile
16 The devil
17 Earthly existence
18 Fidelity, domesticity or lust
19 Greed and lust
20 Humility
21 The Resurrection and salvation
22 Savage passions and excesses
23 Temptation and sin
24 Laziness and lust
25 Diligence and good order

Page 50

1 Joseph Mallord William Turner
2 Vittore Carpaccio
3 Hans Memlinc
4 Anton Romako
5 Jacques Laurent Agasse
6 Paul Signac
7 Giovanni Bellini
8 Jan Steen
9. Giovanni Segantini
10 Albrecht Altdorfer
11 Hans Baldung Grien
12 Willem II van der Velde
13 Stanley Spencer
14 Gillian Ayres
15 Sawrey Gilpin
16 Gerard Terborch
17 Joseph-Marie Vien
18 Édouard Manet
19 Frans Post
20 Andrea del Castagno
21 Marco Basaiti
22 Berthe Morisot
23 Frans Floris
24 Pierre Puvis de Chavannes
25 Gavin Hamilton

Page 51

1 "The Rokeby Venus" by Diego Velazquez
2 "The Monarch of the Glen" by Edwin Landseer
3 "Impression: Sunrise" by Claude Monet (Musée Marmottan, Paris)
4 "The Cenotaph" (National Gallery, London)
5 "The Ambassadors of Agamemnon in the Tent of Achilles" (École des Beaux-Arts, Paris)
6 "The Raising of Lazarus" by Sebastiano del Piombo
7 "Nocturne in Black and Gold: The Falling Rocket" (Institute of Art, Detroit)
8 "The Mona Lisa" by Leonardo
9 "Christ in the House of His Parents" by John Everett Millais (Tate Gallery, London)
10 "Life at the Seaside (Ramsgate Sands)" by William Powell Frith (The Royal Collection)
11 "Landscape with Hagar and the Angel" by Claude Lorraine (National Gallery, London)
12 "The Santa Trinità Madonna" by Cimabue (Uffizi, Florence)
13 "Bubbles" by John Everett Millais
14 "The Raft of the Medusa" by Théodore Géricault (Louvre, Paris)
15 "The Portrait of Sir Winston Churchill" by Graham Sutherland (commissioned by an all-party committee of both Houses of Parliament as a present for his eightieth birthday)
16 "The Derby Day" by William Powell Frith (Tate Gallery, London)
17 "Dolbaddern Castle, North Wales"
18 "The Transfiguration" by Raphael (Pinacoteca Vatican)
19 "Guernica" by Picasso (Museo Nacional Reina Sofia, Madrid)
20 "The Feast of the Gods" (National Gallery of Art, Washington)
21 "The Hay-Wain" by John Constable (National Gallery, London)
22 "The Night Watch" by Rembrandt (Rijksmuseum, Amsterdam)
23 "Pegwell Bay, Kent" by William Dyce (Tate Gallery, London)
24 "The Surrender of Breda" by Diego Velazquez (Prado, Madrid)
25 "Strayed Sheep" by William Holman Hunt (Tate Gallery, London)

Page 52

1 Philip James de Loutherbourg
2 Thomas Lawrence
3 Hans von Marées
4 William Hodges
5 Ary Scheffer
6 Richard Diebenkorn
7 Luca Giordano
8 Edwin Austin Abbey
9 Willem Mesdag
10 Juan de Pareja
11 Perino del Vaga
12 Federico Barocci
13 Jules Bastien-Lepage
14 Mark Rothko
15 Lucio Fontana
16 William Dyce
17 Andrea del Castagno
18 Jan van Scorel
19 Otto Dix
20 Henry Fuseli
21 Thomas Lawrence
22 Andrea Sacchi
23 Fra Bartolommeo
24 Giovanni Fattori
25 Nicholas Hilliard

Page 53

1 Humility
2 The Holy Spirit or the Seven Joys and Seven Sorrows of the Virgin
3 Purity
4 Martyrdom
5 The Passion
6 Sorrow and death
7 Betrothal. Three red carnations symbolize the blood-stained nails of the Passion
8 Sleep and death. It is also a symbol of the Passion
9 Christian prudence
10 The Trinity
11 Earthly sorrow and sin. It is also a symbol of the Passion
12 Wickedness invading the Church
13 The Virgin Mary
14 The Passion and the sorrow in Mary's heart
15 Unswerving Christian faith
16 The Gentiles converted by Christ
17 Penitence and humility. It also symbolizes the Baptism
18 Remembrance and meditation
19 Purity
20 Immortality
21 The innocence of the Infant Christ
22 The triumph of divine love over death
23 The Virgin's sorrow at the death of Christ
24 Eternal life
25 The Advent of Christ

Page 54

1 Henri Fantin-Latour
2 Caravaggio
3 John Martin
4 Jacques-Louis David
5 Hans Memlinc
6 Raphael
7 Pierre Auguste Renoir
8 Nicolas Poussin
9 Joseph Mallord William Turner
10 David Hockney
11 Hugo van der Goes
12 Eugène Delacroix
13 Jean Fouquet
14 Joseph Wright of Derby
15 Piero di Cosimo
16 Josef Albers
17 David Wilkie
18 Giorgione
19 Bartolomé Estebán Murillo
20 John Everett Millais
21 James Ward
22 Kasimir Malevich
23 El Greco
24 Albrecht Dürer
25 Ilya Repin

Page 55

1 Kenneth Clark
2 Walter F. Friedländer
3 Erwin Panofsky
4 Frederick Antal
5 Erwin Panofsky
6 Max J. Friedlaender
7 Francis D. Klingender
8 Grete Ring
9 William T. Whitley
10 Jean Seznec
11 Erwin Panofsky
12 John Rewald
13 Edgar Wind
14 Frederick Antal
15 Arnold Hauser
16 Robert J. Goldwater
17 Walter F. Friedländer
18 Millard Meiss
19 John Canaday
20 John Pope-Hennessy
21 Nikolaus Pevsner
22 Gustav F. Waagen
24 Francis Haskell
24 Denis Mahon
25 John White

Page 56

1 An ass, a heron, and a flock of sheep
2 A dog
3 Three dogs and a monkey
4 A sheep and two lambs
5 A cormorant, a pelican, a snake, and cattle
6 A wolf, a lion, and a dog
7 Two peacocks, a magpie, and a goldfinch
8 An ox, an ass, a magpie, and two goldfinches
9 A cat
10 A dog
11 Two horses and a peacock
12 A dog and two squirrels
13 Horses, dogs, a stag, and a swan
14 A partridge, a peacock, and a lion
15 A cormorant, two pelicans, and four rabbits
16 An ox, an ass, and a lamb
17 A dog, a cat, an ox, and a cockerel
18 A ram
19 A monkey, a bear, a donkey, a sow, five piglets, and a duck
20 A horse and three camels
21 A young bull, a cow, a ram, a sheep, a lamb, a frog, and a skylark
22 A dog, a hare, two swans, two goldfinches, and a woodpecker
23 A dove and a partridge
24 A cat
25 An ass, a dog, and two leopards

Page 57

1 Prudence, piety or chastity
2 Christ's Passion
3 Immortality
4 The Resurrection
5 Purity and peace. It also symbolizes the Holy Spirit
6 The Devil
7 Sorrow
8 Humility
9 Watchfulness and vigilance
10 Sin or lust
11 Wisdom and solitude. It also symbolizes Satan, the Prince of Darkness
12 The meek and the lowly
13 Christ's Sacrifice on the Cross
14 The Incarnation of Christ
15 Heresy. It also symbolizes the Devil
16 Vigilance and loyalty
17 *Either* the Church and truth *or* deceit, theft and the Devil
18 Providence and vigilance
19 The Resurrection. It also represents the inspiration of the gospels
20 Sin and the temptations of the flesh
21 Evil thought or action
22 The Gentile converted to Christianity
23 The Resurrection and the triumph of eternal life over death
24 Hope
25 The soul

117

Page 58

1 Horatio McCulloch
2 Gustave Courbet
3 Herri met de Bles
4 Claude Lorraine
5 Meindert Hobbema
6 Vincent van Gogh
7 Salvator Rosa
8 Adam Elsheimer
9 Thomas Gainsborough
10 Paul Cézanne
11 Victor Pasmore
12 Joseph Anton Koch
13 Ford Madox Brown
14 Paul Nash
15 Samuel Palmer
16 Camille Pissarro
17 Claude Monet
18 Peter Paul Rubens
19 John Constable
20 Caspar David Friedrich
21 Jacob More
22 El Greco
23 John Brett
24 Nicolas Poussin
25 Claude Monet

Page 59

1 Dante Gabriel Rossetti
2 Botticelli
3 Édouard Manet
4 Raphael
5 Philipp Otto Runge
6 Vincent van Gogh
7 Botticelli
8 Thomas Eakins
9 Jean-Auguste-Dominique Ingres
10 Ferdinand Hodler
11 Leonardo da Vinci
12 Rosa Bonheur
13 Titian
14 Paul Nash
15 Hans Eworth
16 Raphael
17 John Singleton Copley
18 Jean Fouquet
19 Edward Coley Burne-Jones
20 Georges Seurat
21 Anne Louis Girodet
22 William Hogarth
23 Pierre Auguste Renoir
24 Gino Severini
25 Raphael

Page 60

1 English painter of American parentage; friend and biographer of John Constable
2 French painter of still-lifes in the manner of Jean-Baptiste-Siméon Chardin
3 Dutch forger of pictures purporting to be by Jan Vermeer, Pieter de Hooch and others
4 Wife of Giovanni Arnolfini
5 Founder, in 1766, of the London auction house Christies
6 Cologne banker who purchased many of the paintings from the collection of Charles I and resold them to, among others, Louis XIV
7 The wife and frequent model of Salvador Dali
8 English collector, whose pictures formed the nucleus of the National Gallery in London following their purchase by the Government in 1824
9 Poet and philosopher at the Medici court in Florence
10 Partner in an Amsterdam weaving company; burgomaster of Amsterdam; and patron and benefactor of Rembrandt
11 French picture dealer and publisher, champion of the avant-garde; supporter of Cézanne, Gauguin and the early Cubists
12 Pupil and imitator of Frans Hals
13 American writer, early patron of Picasso, Braque and Cézanne
14 French philosopher and critic; editor (with d'Alembert) of the famous Encyclopédie; author of important reviews of the Salons which are the origins of modern art criticism
15 American patron and art dealer; founder in 1942 of The art of this Century Gallery in New York; owner of the art collection in Venice which bears her name
16 Bristol-born pioneer of motion photography of decisive influence on the Impressionists, the Futurists and others
17 Dancer at the Moulin Rouge, Le Divan Japonais and Le Jardin de Paris; frequently depicted in paintings and lithographs by Henri de Toulouse-Lautrec
18 English painter, art historian and arts administrator; President of the Royal Academy (1850-1865); appointed Director of the National Gallery (1855)
19 Italian engraver, particularly associated with Raphael
20 French doctor who attended Vincent van Gogh
21 Italian painter, collector and dealer in antiquities; teacher of Andrea Mantegna and Marco Zoppo
22 Friend and patron of Gustave Courbet
23 Miniaturist; illustrator of the Farnese Book of Hours; confidant of El Greco
24 Painter and broadcaster, accused of forgery
25 The wife of Allan Ramsay

Page 61
1 David Wilkie
2 Joan Miró
3 Diego Velazquez
4 Titian
5 John Constable
6 Antonio Correggio
7 Caspar David Friedrich
8 El Greco
9 Andrea Mantegna
10 Michelangelo
11 Jean-Auguste-Dominique Ingres
12 Hans Holbein the Younger
13 James McNeill Whistler
14 Salvador Dali
15 Edgar Degas
16 Benjamin West
17 Rembrandt
18 Thomas Gainsborough
19 Claude Monet
20 Vincent van Gogh
21 Matthias Grünewald
22 Édouard Manet
23 Anthony van Dyck
24 Pontormo
25 Mary Cassatt

Page 62
1 Jacques-Louis David
2 Malcolm Morley
3 Andy Warhol
4 Benjamin West
5 Gustave Courbet
6 Antoine Gros
7 Paolo Veronese
8 Bamboccio (Pieter van Laer)
9 Paul Cézanne
10 Peter Lely
11 Albrecht Altdorfer
12 Paul Sérusier
13 Alexander Cozens
14 Rosalba Carriera
15 Edward Lear
16 James McNeill Whistler
17 Antoine Gros
18 Mary Moser
19 Joshua Reynolds
20 Théodore Chassériau
21 William Blake
22 Thomas Gainsborough
23 Francesco Zuccarelli
24 Josef Albers
25 Dante Gabriel Rossetti

Page 63
1 The Master of Flémalle (Robert Campin)
2 Pierre-Narcisse Guérin
3 Pietro Perugino
4 Simone Peterzano
5 Francisco Pacheco
6 Michael Wolgemut
7 Carel van Mander
8 Piero di Cosimo
9 Hendrick van Balen
10 François Lemoyne
11 Andrea del Verrocchio
12 Pieter Coecke van Aelst
13 Hans Holbein the Elder
14 Agostino Tassi
15 Jacob Isaacz Swanenburgh and Pieter Lastman
16 Cimabue
17 Rembrandt
18 Ferdinand Bol
19 Giovanni Bellini
20 Jacques-Louis David
21 Duccio
22 Adam van Noort
23 Juan del Castillo
24 Botticelli
25 Thomas Hudson

Page 64
1 Father and son
2 Uncle and nephew
3 Brother and sister
4 Brothers-in-law
5 Brothers
6 Husband and wife
7 Brothers
8 Father and daughter
9 Husband and wife
10 Brothers
11 Uncle and nephew
12 Father and son
13 Brother-in-law and sister-in-law
14 Father and son
15 Uncle and nephew
16 Father and son
17 Father-in-law and son-in-law
18 Father and son
19 Husband and wife
20 Husband and wife
21 Mother and son
22 Father and son
23 Brothers
24 Husband and wife
25 Brothers-in-law

Page 79

1 1629
2 1892
3 1577
4 1663
5 1852
6 1911
7 1914
8 1624
9 1625
10 1855
11 1460
12 1857
13 1903
14 1667
15 1876
16 1774
17 1891
18 1779
19 1868
20 1627
21 1884
22 1712
23 1879
24 1883
25 1911

Page 80

1 Giulio Romano
2 Gregorio de Ferrari
3 Giotto
4 Andrea Mantegna
5 Pierre Puvis de Chavannes
6 Johann Michael Rottmayr
7 Andrea del Castagno
8 Stanley Spencer
9 Raphael
10 Michelangelo
11 Vincenzo Foppa
12 Domenico Ghirlandaio
13 Antonio Correggio
14 Giorgione
15 Luca Signorelli
16 James Barry
17 Piero della Francesca
18 Pietro Perugino
19 Francesco del Cossa
20 Andrea Mantegna
21 Louis Laguerre
22 François Lemoyne
23 Filippo Lippi
24 Luca Giordano
25 Fra Angelico

Page 81

1 Lorenzo di Pierfrancesco de' Medici
2 Jodocus and/or Elisabeth Vijd
3 Philip II of Spain
4 Enrico Scrovegni
5 Chancellor Nicholas Rolin
6 Charles III of Spain
7 The Emperor Rudolf II
8 Tommaso Portinari
9 Clement VII and then Pope Paul III
10 Paul Fréart de Chantelou
11 Federigo II Gonzaga
12 Philip II of Spain
13 Laerzio Cherubin of Norcia
14 François I, King of France
15 Caroline Murat, Queen of Naples
16 Alfonso d'Este
17 Cardinal Odoardo Farnese
18 Philip IV of Spain
19 Pope Julius II
20 The Grand Duke of Tuscany
21 Lorenzo Cardoni (?)
22 Piero de' Medici (the Gouty)
23 Ludovico Gonzaga
24 Alfonso d'Este
25 Constantijn Huygens on behalf of the Prince of Orange

Page 82

1 1793
2 1624
3 1586
4 1529
5 1689
6 1907
7 1285
8 1652
9 1498
10 1830
11 1501
12 1885
13 1656
14 1333
15 1533
16 1821
17 1872
18 1434
19 1520
20 1821
21 1505
22 1785
23 1911
24 1423
25 1888

Page 83

1 Pontormo
2 Baciccio or Baciccia
3 Master of the Housebook
4 Giulio Romano
5 Gaspare Vanvitelli
6 Giovanni Benedetto Castiglione
7 Wols
8 Sebastiano del Piombo
9 Melozzo da Forlì
10 Emil Nolde
11 Justus of Ghent
12 Orcagna
13 Pietro da Cortona
14 Mattia Preti
15 Mihály Munkácsy
16 Cornelis van Haarlem
17 Piero della Francesca
18 Dosso Dossi
19 Balthus
20 Pisanello
21 Beccafumi
22 Masolino
23 Domenico Veneziano
24 Jacopo Bassano
25 Piero di Cosimo

Page 84

1 Jean-Auguste-Dominique Ingres
2 Franz Marc
3 John Singleton Copley
4 Edvard Munch
5 Benjamin West
6 Salvador Dali
7 Théodore Géricault
8 Henri Matisse
9 Joseph Mallord William Turner
10 Giacomo Balla
11 Edwin Landseer
12 Édouard Manet
13 Max Ernst
14 Arthur Hughes
15 Charles Demuth
16 Vincent van Gogh
17 Edward Hopper
18 Gustave Caillebotte
19 Hubert von Herkomer
20 Paul Gauguin
21 Paul Cézanne
22 Wilhelm Leibl
23 Fernand Léger
24 Gwen John
25 Anthony van Dyck

Page 85

1 The Palais du Luxembourg, Paris
2 The Palazzo Medici-Riccardi, Florence
3 The Hospital of St Anthony at Isenheim, near Colmar
4 The Studiolo of Alfonso d'Este in Ferrara
5 The Church of S. Sisto, Rome
6 The Cathedral, Siena
7 The Church of S. Maria Novella, Florence
8 The Church of St Walburga, Antwerp
9 The Church of S. Maria della Scala, Trastevere
10 The Scuola di San Marco, Venice
11 The refectory of SS. Giovanni e Paolo, Venice
12 The Great Hall of the Musketeers' Guild in Amsterdam
13 The Salón de los Reinos of the Buen Retiro Palace, Madrid
14 The Antwerp villa of Niclaes Jonghelinck
15 The Church of Ognissanti, Florence
16 The house of Lorenzo di Pierfrancesco de' Medici, next to the Palazzo Medici in Florence
17 The Ducal Palace, Urbino
18 The Camerino d'Alabastro of Duke Alfonso d'Este of Ferrara
19 The Camerino of Isabella d'Este in the Castello of Mantua
20 The Munich Residenz of Duke Wilhelm IV of Bavaria
21 The Pucci Chapel of SS. Annunziata in Florence
22 The Chatreuse de Champmol in Dijon
23 The chapel of the hospital of S. Maria Nuova in Florence
24 The Church of S. Trinità in Florence
25 The exact position in the Accademia which it still occupies

Page 86

1 Cristofano Allori
2 Marc Chagall
3 Peter Blake
4 Oskar Kokoschka
5 Albrecht Dürer
6 Francisco Goya
7 Carel Fabritius
8 James Barry
9 Joshua Reynolds
10 William Hogarth
11 Jean Fouquet
12 Parmigianino
13 Max Beckmann
14 Caravaggio
15 Hans von Marées
16 Gustave Courbet
17 Marten van Heemskerck
18 Ernst Ludwig Kirchner
19 Charles Willson Peale
20 Paul Gauguin
21 Rembrandt
22 Lovis Corinth
23 Anthony van Dyck
24 Francisco de Zurbarán
25 Vincent van Gogh

Page 87

1 Philip IV of Spain
2 François I (King of France)
3 The Emperor Maximilian I and the Emperor Charles V
4 Philip the Bold, Duke of Burgundy
5 Henri II and Charles IX (Kings of France)
6 Cosimo I de' Medici, first Grand Duke of Tuscany
7 Charles I (King of England)
8 Friedrich August II of Saxony
9 The Emperor Rudolf II
10 Henry VIII (King of England)
11 Philip the Good, Duke of Burgundy
12 Ferdinando Gonzaga, Duke of Mantua
13 Queen Christina of Sweden
14 The Spanish Governors of the Netherlands
15 Marie de' Medici
16 Charles I (King of England)
17 Isabella d'Este
18 Louis XV (King of France)
19 Johann Wilhelm, Elector of the Palatinate
20 Frederick the Wise, Elector of Saxony and his two successors
21 King Ferdinand and Queen Isabella of Spain
22 Charles IV (King of Spain)
23 The Empress Josephine and the Empress Marie Louise of France
24 Philip II (King of Spain)
25 The Emperor Maximilian I

Page 88

1 Pedro Diaz de Villanueva
2 Pieter Bruegel the Younger
3 Paul Delaroche
4 Piero della Francesca
5 Fra Filippo Lippi
6 Domenico Veneziano
7 Francesco Squarcione
8 Andrea del Sarto
9 Domenico Ghirlandaio
10 Innocenzo da Imola
11 Denys Calvaert
12 Andrea del Verrocchio
13 Adam van Noort and Otto van Veen
14 Thomas Couture
15 Cosimo Rosselli
16 José Luzán
17 Alexandre Lenoir
18 Rembrandt
19 David Teniers the Elder
20 Raffaelino del Garbo and Pontormo
21 Quentin Varin
22 Agostino Carracci
23 Pierre Jacques Cazes and Noël Coypel
24 Alphonse Legros
25 Francesco Imperiali and Francesco Solimena

Page 90

1 Peter Paul Rubens
2 Gentile Bellini
3 Thomas Lawrence
4 Charles Willson Peale
5 Georges Rouault
6 Percy Wyndham Lewis
7 Rosso Fiorentino
8 Andries Both
9 Thomas Sandby
10 Honoré Daumier
11 John Crome
12 Joshua Reynolds
13 David Allan
14 Mariotto Albertinelli
15 Benjamin Marshall
16 Giuseppe Arcimboldo
17 Nicolaes Berchem
18 Mary Cassatt
19 Walter Richard Sickert
20 Federico Zuccari
21 Robert Henri
22 Charles Lebrun
23 John Opie
24 Augustus John
25 Gerhard von Kügelgen

Page 91

1 Brazil
2 Venice
3 France
4 Algeria
5 Düsseldorf
6 Rome
7 Prague
8 Urbino
9 Copenhagen
10 Paris
11 Rome
12 Rome
13 USA
14 Bologna
15 Nuremberg
16 Mexico
17 Rome
18 England
19 Munich
20 Pontoise
21 Paris
22 USA
23 Rome
24 Italy
25 London

Page 92

1 1951
2 1827
3 1422
4 1644
5 1943
6 1661
7 1888
8 1425
9 1763
10 1473
11 1682
12 1479
13 1518
14 1894
15 1465
16 1596
17 1488
18 1492
19 1548
20 1600
21 1866
22 1774
23 1557
24 1421
25 1905

Page 93

1 Uccello
2 Tintoretto
3 Titian
4 Masaccio
5 Verrocchio
6 Mathias Grünewald
7 Fra Angelico
8 Caravaggio
9 Veronese
10 Theo van Doesburg
11 El Greco
12 Fra Bartolommeo
13 Guercino
14 Bronzino
15 Domenichino
16 Palma Giovane
17 Orazio Gentileschi
18 Giorgione
19 Botticelli
20 Canaletto
21 Cimabue
22 Parmigianino
23 Sodoma
24 Domenico Ghirlandaio
25 Antonio Correggio

Page 94

1 1610
2 1565
3 1771
4 1800
5 1812
6 1943
7 1573
8 1819
9 1948
10 1740
11 1662
12 1814
13 1824
14 1526
15 1847
16 1849
17 1889
18 1810
19 1820
20 1717
21 1872
22 1893
23 1481
24 1850
25 1659

Page 95

1 Claude Lorraine
2 George Augustus Wallis
3 Aubrey Beardsley
4 Alexander Cozens
5 Paul Cézanne
6 Thomas Gainsborough
7 Leonardo
8 Percy Wyndham Lewis
9 Roy Lichtenstein
10 Hans Memlinc
11 Michelangelo
12 John Everett Millais
13 Claude Monet
14 Jackson Pollock
15 Giovanni Battista Tiepolo
16 Jacopo Tintoretto
17 Jan Vermeer
18 Richard Wilson
19 Hans Memlinc
20 Hieronymus Bosch
21 William Blake
22 Paul Nash
23 Yves Tanguy
24 El Greco
25 Fra Angelico

Page 96

1 Uncle and nephew
2 Father and son
3 Father-in-law and son-in-law
4 Husband and wife
5 Brothers-in-law
6 Uncle and nephew
7 Father and son
8 Brother-in-law and sister-in-law
9 Brothers-in-law
10 Brothers-in-law
11 Husband and wife
12 Uncle and nephew
13 Father and son
14 Father-in-law and son-in-law
15 Brothers
16 Cousins
17 Father and son
18 Father-in-law and son-in-law
19 Brothers
20 Brothers
21 Brother and sister
22 Brothers
23 Father and son
24 Father and son
25 Brothers

Page 97

1 Elizabeth Siddal
2 Saskia van Uylenburch
3 The artist Marcellin Desboutin and Ellen Andrée, an actress
4 Berthe Morisot
5 Mrs William Morris (Jane Burden)
6 The artist himself
7 The critic F. G. Stephens
8 Susanna Fourment, the sister of the artist's second wife, Hélène
9 Thomas Carlyle
10 Thomas Lister, later 1st Earl Ribblesdale
11 The artist's brother Edmond and a professional model known as Nini or Gueule-de-Raie
12 Victor Jacquemont
13 The artist and his favourite pupil August Heinrich
14 W. J. Stillman
15 George Meredith
16 Don Diego de Acedo
17 The artist's wife
18 Hélène Fourment
19 Jonathan Buttall
20 Eugène Delacroix
21 Connie Gilchrist, a skipping-rope dancer who later married the Earl of Orkney
22 Christina Olsen
23 The artist's son, Jorge Manuel
24 The artist's wife
25 Mme Augustine Roulin

Page 98

1 Marten van Heemskerck
2 Gwen John
3 Nicolas Poussin
4 Ernest Meissonier
5 Vincent van Gogh
6 Michelangelo
7 Albrecht Dürer
8 Caravaggio
9 Antonio Correggio
10 Hans Holbein the Younger
11 Joos van Cleve
12 Titian
13 Guercino
14 Claude Lorraine
15 Édouard Manet
16 Diego Velazquez
17 Baciccio (Giovanni Battista Gaulli)
18 Bartolomé Estebán Murillo
19 Jan Miense Molenaer
20 Peter Paul Rubens
21 Guido Reni
22 Titian
23 Maurice Utrillo
24 Jan Vermeer
25 Salvador Dali

COMPETITION

The answers to the following five questions are not provided at the end of the book like all the others, but clues to some of the solutions lie somewhere within The Art Quiz Book itself.

Questions:

1. For which Pope did Michelangelo execute the frescoes on the ceiling of the Sistine Chapel
2. In which gallery is Diego Velazquez's "Surrender of Breda"
3. Whose pupil was the painter Judith Leyster
4. Whose portrait of Sir Winston Churchill was allegedly destroyed by the sitter's widow
5. Between which years is "The Wilton Diptych" believed to have been painted

Once you have the five answers, write them on a postcard together with your name and address and send it to:-

The Art Quiz Book Competition
Station Press Ltd
10 Links Place
Port Seton
East Lothian
EH32 0TP

The senders of the first five correct solutions, drawn at random each quarter, will each receive a print of Agnolo Bronzino's "An Allegory of Venus, Cupid, Folly and Time", which is reproduced on the front cover of The Art Quiz Book.

We will also put your name on our mailing list, and keep you informed of future publications.

If you wish your name to be put on our mailing list, but do not want to enter the competition, please send a postcard with your name and address to our Customer Update Department at the above address.

A junior edition of The Art Quiz Book will be available shortly, and editions with different questions and subjects are also being planned for future publication. The Art Quiz Book will also be available in computer software format soon. Full details of these and other publications will be forwarded to you by our Customer Update Department from time to time.

Notes

Notes

Notes